Editorial project:
© 2025 **booq** publishing, S.L.
c/ Domènech, 7-9, 2º 1ª
08012 Barcelona, Spain
T: +34 93 268 80 88
www.booqpublishing.com

ISBN: 978-84-9936-569-5 [EN]
ISBN: 978-84-9936-568-8 [ES]

© Éditions du Layeur
Dépôt Légal : Juin 2025
Espagne, en juin 2025

ISBN : 978-2-38378-088-5

Editorial coordinator:
Claudia Martínez Alonso

Art director:
Sergio Asensio Quesada

Editor:
Daniela Santos Quartino
David Andreu Bach

Layout:
Cristina Simó Perales

Translation:
© **booq** publishing, S.L.

Printing in China

ARCHITECTURE AND INTERIORS FOR A GENTLE LIFE

The slow home is more than just design, it's a mindset. Rooted in intention, calm, and authenticity, it blends architecture, interiors, and lifestyle into a harmonious whole. Soft materials, natural light, and mindful choices shape spaces that nurture well-being. It's about living gently, embracing the moment, and creating homes that feel grounded, human, and quietly powerful.

A tender and timely reflection on how we live the concept Slow Home reminds us that beauty lies in simplicity, care, and intention. A soulful book for those seeking refuge, rhythm, and deeper connection through design.

This beautiful book is a visual and emotional journey through spaces designed to slow us down. Blending architecture, interior design, and lifestyle, the book celebrates projects that prioritize calm, connection, and presence. These are homes—not houses—created with care, where every element serves a purpose and reflects the people who live there. From earthy materials and thoughtful layouts to rituals of daily life, the slow home is about beauty that's lived, not displayed.

This edition brings together international projects that embody this philosophy, offering inspiration for a more grounded, intentional way of living. In an age of speed and noise, The Slow Home offers a sanctuary of stillness, grace, and mindful design.

ARCHITEKTUR UND INNENEINRICHTUNG FÜR EIN RUHIGES LEBEN

Das Slow-Home-Konzept ist mehr als nur Design, es ist eine Denkweise. Es basiert auf Absicht, Ruhe und Authentizität und verbindet Architektur, Inneneinrichtung und Lebensstil zu einem harmonischen Ganzen. Weiche Materialien, natürliches Licht und bewusste Entscheidungen schaffen Räume, die das Wohlbefinden fördern. Es geht um ein sanftes Leben, um die Umarmung und Schaffung von Häusern, die sich geerdet, menschlich und ruhig kraftvoll anfühlen.

Das Slow Home-Konzept ist eine zärtliche und zeitgemäße Reflexion darüber, wie wir leben, und erinnert uns daran, dass Schönheit in Einfachheit, Sorgfalt und Absicht liegt. Ein Buch für alle, die Zuflucht, Rhythmus und eine tiefere Verbindung durch Design suchen.

Dieser wunderschöne Band ist eine visuelle und emotionale Reise durch Räume, die uns entschleunigen sollen. Das Buch verbindet Architektur, Innenarchitektur und Lifestyle und stellt Projekte vor, die Ruhe, Verbindung und Präsenz in den Vordergrund stellen. Es sind Wohnungen - nicht Häuser - die mit Sorgfalt geschaffen wurden, in denen jedes Element eine Funktion hat und die Menschen widerspiegelt, die darin leben. Von erdigen Materialien über durchdachtes Design bis hin zu den Ritualen des täglichen Lebens - bei Slow Home geht es um Schönheit, die gelebt und nicht zur Schau gestellt wird.

Diese Ausgabe bringt internationale Projekte zusammen, die diese Philosophie verkörpern und Inspiration für eine bewusstere und bewusstere Lebensweise bieten. In einem Zeitalter der Geschwindigkeit und des Lärms bietet Slow Home einen Zufluchtsort der Stille, der Anmut und des bewussten Designs.

ARCHITECTURE ET INTÉRIEURS POUR UNE VIE PAISIBLE

Le concept Slow Home est plus qu'un simple design, c'est un état d'esprit. Basé sur l'intention, le calme et l'authenticité, il associe l'architecture, les intérieurs et le style de vie en un tout harmonieux. Des matériaux doux, la lumière naturelle et des choix réfléchis créent des espaces qui favorisent le bien-être. Il s'agit de vivre en douceur, d'embrasser et de créer des maisons qui se sentent enracinées, humaines et tranquillement puissantes.

Une réflexion tendre et opportune sur notre façon de vivre, le concept de Slow Home nous rappelle que la beauté réside dans la simplicité, l'attention et l'intention. Un livre pour ceux qui cherchent un refuge, un rythme et une connexion plus profonde à travers le design.

Ce magnifique volume est un voyage visuel et émotionnel à travers des espaces conçus pour nous ralentir. Combinant architecture, design d'intérieur et style de vie, ce livre célèbre des projets qui privilégient le calme, la connexion et la présence. Il s'agit de maisons - et non d'habitations - créées avec soin, où chaque élément a une fonction et reflète les personnes qui y vivent. Des matériaux naturels aux rituels de la vie quotidienne, en passant par des designs réfléchis, Slow Home met en avant une beauté qui se vit et ne s'exhibe pas.

Cette édition rassemble des projets internationaux qui incarnent cette philosophie et offrent une inspiration pour un mode de vie plus conscient et intentionnel. À l'ère de la vitesse et du bruit, Slow Home offre un sanctuaire de calme, de grâce et de design conscient.

ARQUITECTURA E INTERIORES PARA UNA VIDA TRANQUILA

El concepto Slow Home es algo más que diseño, es una mentalidad. Basada en la intención, la calma y la autenticidad, combina arquitectura, interiores y estilo de vida en un todo armonioso. Materiales suaves, luz natural y elecciones conscientes conforman espacios que fomentan el bienestar. Se trata de vivir con suavidad, abrazar y crear hogares que se sientan arraigados, humanos y silenciosamente poderosos.

Una reflexión tierna y oportuna sobre cómo vivimos el concepto Slow Home nos recuerda que la belleza reside en la sencillez, el cuidado y la intención. Un libro para quienes buscan refugio, ritmo y una conexión más profunda a través del diseño.

Este hermoso volumen es un viaje visual y emocional a través de espacios diseñados para ralentizarnos. Combinando arquitectura, diseño de interiores y estilo de vida, el libro celebra proyectos que priorizan la calma, la conexión y la presencia. Son hogares —no casas— creados con esmero, en los que cada elemento tiene una función y refleja a las personas que viven en ellos. Desde los materiales terrosos y los diseños reflexivos hasta los rituales de la vida cotidiana, Slow Home es la belleza que se vive, no la que se exhibe.

Esta edición reúne proyectos internacionales que encarnan esta filosofía y ofrecen inspiración para una forma de vida más consciente e intencionada. En una era de velocidad y ruido, Slow Home ofrece un santuario de quietud, gracia y diseño consciente.

Muskoka, Ontario, Canada

MUSKOKA COTTAGE

A cedar-clad cottage nestled in Ontario's rugged landscape, where refined minimalism and warm interiors create a peaceful lakeside retreat.

This multi-generational family cottage is clad in rough-sawn cedar boards and western red cedar shakes to blend seamlessly with the northern Ontario terrain of windswept trees and Pre-Cambrian bedrock. The 7,500-square-foot residence is comprised of three interconnected volumes, crafting an interior characterized by both cozy spaces and open rooms, each providing spectacular views of a fresh-water lake. The interior finishes emphasize the elemental, with bespoke concrete vanities and kitchen cabinetry discreetly integrated into the wood wall boards and aligned flush with the island's granite countertop. Soft furnishings, selected by Ashley Botten Design, and area rugs in neutral tones add warmth to the architectural interplay between rustic charm and finely crafted minimalism.
Siting the main volume on a naturally sloped elevation allowed for a lower level with a walk-out. A cedar sauna, fitness room, and recreation room are steps away from pathways leading to the boathouse and shoreline.

Cabine Muskoka, cette cabane familiale multigénérationnelle revêtue de planches de cèdre sciées et de tuiles de cèdre rouge occidental se fond avec le paysage du nord de l'Ontario, où les arbres sont balayés par le vent et la roche mère précambrienne. La résidence de 697 mètres carrés comprend trois volumes interconnectés qui forment un intérieur de espaces accueillants et de chambres ouvertes avec des vues spectaculaires sur un lac d'eau douce. Les finitions intérieures se concentrent sur l'élémentaire, avec des vanités en béton sur mesure et des armoires de cuisine conçues pour se fondre dans les planches murales et courir à ras avec le comptoir en granit de l'îlot. Le mobilier, sélectionné par Ashley Botten Design, et les tapis dans des tons neutres ajoutent de la chaleur à l'interaction architecturale entre le charme rustique et l'artisanat minimaliste.
Placer le volume principal sur une élévation naturelle a permis un niveau inférieur avec sortie. Un sauna en cèdre, une salle de fitness et une salle de jeux sont à quelques pas des sentiers menant à l'embarcadère et au rivage.

Diese multigenerationale Familienhütte, verkleidet mit gesägten Zedernbrettern und westlichen roten Zedernschindeln, verschmilzt mit der Landschaft im Norden von Ontario, wo Bäume vom Wind gepeitscht werden und präkambrischer Mutterfels liegt. Die 697 m^2 große Residenz besteht aus drei miteinander verbundenen Volumen, die ein gemütliches Interieur und Zimmer mit spektakulärem Blick auf einen Süßwassersee bilden. Die Innenausstattung konzentriert sich auf das Elementare, mit maßgefertigten Betonwaschtischen und Küchenschränken, die so gestaltet sind, dass sie in die Wandverkleidungen übergehen und bündig mit der Granit-Arbeitsplatte der Insel abschließen. Von Ashley Botten Design ausgewählte Möbel und Teppiche in neutralen Tönen sorgen für Wärme, rustikalen Charme und minimalistische Handwerkskunst.
Die Platzierung des Hauptvolumens auf einer natürlichen Anhöhe ermöglichte ein unteres Niveau mit Ausgang. Eine Sauna aus Zedernholz, ein Fitnessraum und ein Spielzimmer befinden sich nur wenige Schritte von den Pfaden entfernt, die zum Bootssteg und zum Ufer führen.

Esta cabaña familiar multigeneracional, revestida con tablas de cedro aserrado y tejas de cedro rojo occidental, se fusiona con el terreno del norte de Ontario de árboles azotados por el viento y roca madre precámbrica. La residencia, de 697 m^2 comprende tres volúmenes interconectados que forman un interior de espacios acogedores y habitaciones abiertas con vistas espectaculares a un lago de agua dulce. Los acabados interiores se centran en lo elemental, con vanidades de concreto hechas a medida y gabinetes de cocina hechos para fusionarse con las tablas de pared y correr enrasados con la encimera de granito de la isla. El mobiliario, seleccionado por Ashley Botten Design, y las alfombras en tonos neutros añaden calidez a la interacción arquitectónica entre el encanto rústico y el minimalismo de la artesanía.
Situar el volumen principal en una elevación natural permitió un nivel inferior con salida. Una sauna de cedro, una sala de fitness y una sala de recreo están a pasos de los senderos que conducen al embarcadero y la orilla.

Photos: © Shai Gil, Lauren Miller

AKB ARCHITECTS

Robert Kastelic, Kelly Buffey

Founded in 2004 by Robert Kastelic and Kelly Buffey, Akb Architects is an internationally renowned, Toronto-based residential architecture studio dedicated to the practice and art of building. Akb's design process prioritizes a clarity of vision, attention to detail, and a rigorous commitment to conceptual intent. The prodigious quality of their work is a result of Robert and Kelly's synthesis of architectural, interior and technical design; a comprehensive strategy results in buildings of exceptional resolution and an uncommon level of refinement. A unified and holistic approach to interior and exterior space merges building and landscape into a seamless experience.

Akb Architects wurde 2004 von Robert Kastelic und Kelly Buffey gegründet und ist ein international renommiertes Architekturbüro mit Sitz in Toronto, das sich der Praxis und Kunst des Bauens widmet. Der Entwurfsprozess von Akb legt den Schwerpunkt auf eine klare Vision, die Liebe zum Detail und die konsequente Umsetzung der konzeptionellen Absicht. Die herausragende Qualität ihrer Arbeit ist das Ergebnis von Robert und Kellys Synthese von Architektur, Inneneinrichtung und technischem Design. Eine umfassende Strategie führt zu Gebäuden von außergewöhnlicher Auflösung und einem ungewöhnlichen Maß an Raffinesse. Ein einheitlicher und ganzheitlicher Ansatz für den Innen- und Außenraum lässt Gebäude und Landschaft zu einem nahtlosen Erlebnis verschmelzen.

Fondé en 2004 par Robert Kastelic et Kelly Buffey, Akb Architects est un studio d'architecture résidentielle de renommée internationale, basé à Toronto, qui se consacre à la pratique et à l'art de la construction. Le processus de conception d'Akb Architects donne la priorité à la clarté de la vision, à l'attention portée aux détails et à un engagement rigoureux envers l'intention conceptuelle. La qualité prodigieuse de leur travail est le résultat de la synthèse de Robert et Kelly entre l'architecture, l'intérieur et la conception technique ; une stratégie globale aboutit à des bâtiments d'une résolution exceptionnelle et d'un niveau de raffinement peu commun. Une approche unifiée et holistique de l'espace intérieur et extérieur fusionne le bâtiment et le paysage en une expérience homogène.

Fundado en 2004 por Robert Kastelic y Kelly Buffey, Akb Architects es un estudio de arquitectura residencial de renombre internacional con sede en Toronto dedicado a la construcción. El proceso de diseño de Akb prioriza la claridad de visión, la atención al detalle y un compromiso con la intención conceptual. La calidad de su trabajo es el resultado de la síntesis de diseño arquitectónico, interior y técnico de Robert y Kelly; una estrategia integral que da como resultado edificios de excepcional resolución y un gran nivel de refinamiento. Un enfoque unificado y global del espacio interior y exterior fusiona el edificio y el paisaje en una experiencia sin fisuras.

Elemental materials and soft furnishings combine seamlessly, illustrating Akb Architects' ability to integrate architecture and nature into a harmonious whole.

Pichilemu, Chile

CASA GC

This coastal residence integrates hillside and sea views, blending durable materials and thoughtful spatial design into a harmonious living environment.

The project, led by architect Pía Camus in collaboration with the Altamarea team, emerges from the geographical condition between the hill and the sea. Its location and program distribution adapt to the ravine, taking advantage of the topography to create two ways of living: one at a height with views of the sea and another at a lower level connected to a north-facing patio protected from the wind. Access to the main floor divides the common area from the private one. The bedrooms face west, while the kitchen and dining room open onto a cantilevered north terrace. The ground floor houses the social area, with a living room and barbecue area facing the pool, while the service area is connected to the kitchen by an external staircase. The combination of noble materials stands out: concrete, wood, and iron. Its exposed steel structure outlines the entire perimeter of the facade horizontally. The eucalyptus ceiling extends across its entire surface, providing continuity and warmth to each space.

Le projet, dirigé par l'architecte Pía Camus en collaboration avec l'équipe d'Altamarea, tire parti de la situation géographique entre la colline et la mer. Son emplacement et sa distribution s'adaptent à la gorge en utilisant la topographie pour créer deux façons de vivre : une en hauteur avec vue sur la mer et une autre au niveau inférieur reliée à une cour protégée du vent au nord. L'accès à l'étage principal divise la zone commune de la zone privée. Les chambres sont orientées à l'ouest, tandis que la cuisine et la salle à manger s'ouvrent sur une terrasse nord en porte-à-faux. Le rez-de-chaussée abrite la zone sociale ; salon et auvent face à la piscine, tandis que la zone de service est reliée à la cuisine par un escalier extérieur. La combinaison de matériaux nobles, tels que le béton, le bois et le fer, est remarquable. Sa structure en acier apparent dessine tout le périmètre de la façade horizontalement. Le ciel en eucalyptus se projette sur toute sa surface, apportant continuité et chaleur à chaque espace.

Das von der Architektin Pía Camus in Zusammenarbeit mit dem Team von Altamarea geleitete Projekt entstand aus der geografischen Lage zwischen Hügel und Meer. Die Lage und Verteilung passen sich der Schlucht an und nutzen die Topografie, um zwei Arten des Wohnens zu schaffen: eine in der Höhe mit Blick auf das Meer und eine andere auf niedrigerem Niveau, die mit einem windgeschützten Innenhof verbunden ist. Der Zugang zur Hauptetage trennt den gemeinsamen vom privaten Bereich. Die Schlafzimmer sind nach Westen ausgerichtet, während die Küche und das Esszimmer sich zu einer nördlichen Terrasse mit Überhang öffnen. Das Erdgeschoss beherbergt den sozialen Bereich; Wohnzimmer und Überdachung mit Blick auf den Pool, während der Servicebereich über eine Außentreppe mit der Küche verbunden ist. Besonders hervorzuheben ist die Kombination edler Materialien: Beton, Holz und Eisen. Ihr sichtbares Stahlgerüst zeichnet den gesamten Umfang der Fassade horizontal nach. Die Eukalyptusdecke erstreckt sich über die gesamte Fläche und verleiht jedem Raum Kontinuität und Wärme.

El proyecto, liderado por la arquitecta Pía Camus en colaboración con el equipo de Altamarea, nace a partir de la condición geográfica entre el cerro y el mar. Su emplazamiento y distribución se adaptan a la quebrada aprovechando la topografía para crear dos formas de habitar: una en altura con vistas al mar y otra a nivel inferior conectada con un patio norte protegido del viento. El acceso a la planta principal divide el área común de la privada. Los dormitorios quedan orientados hacia el poniente, mientras la cocina y comedor se abren hacia una terraza norte en voladizo. La planta baja alberga el área social; living y cobertizo frente a la piscina, mientras que el área de servicio se conecta a la cocina por una escalera exterior. Destaca la combinación de materiales nobles: hormigón, madera y hierro. Su estructura de acero a la vista dibuja todo el perímetro de la fachada horizontalmente. El cielo en eucaliptus se proyecta en toda su superficie, aportando continuidad y calidez a cada espacio.

Photos: © Lucía Fernandez

ALTAMAREA ARQUITECTURA

Altamarea Team

Altamarea, an office established in 2015 by architect Gonzalo Herreros and engineer Matias Quinlan, is primarily characterized by its comprehensive development of housing projects and investments for the coastal area of Chile. We develop architecture that suits the location, recognizing the climatic conditions and their variations throughout the year. We build projects with simple materials of local origin, achieving great construction and architectural results.
Based on our beach life experience, we create living experiences focused on energy efficiency, light utilization, and long-lasting durability, key concepts in the development of our projects.

Altamarea ist ein Büro, das im Jahr 2015 vom Architekten Gonzalo Herreros und dem Ingenieur Matias Quinlan gegründet wurde. Es ist hauptsächlich auf die umfassende Entwicklung von Wohnprojekten und Investitionen an der chilenischen Küste spezialisiert. Wir entwickeln eine dem Ort angemessene Architektur, indem wir die klimatischen Bedingungen und ihre Veränderungen im Laufe des Jahres berücksichtigen. Wir bauen Projekte mit einfachen Materialien aus lokaler Herkunft, die zu großartigen Bauelementen und architektonischen Ergebnissen führen.
Basierend auf unserer Lebenserfahrung am Strand schaffen wir für unsere Kunden Lebenserfahrungen, die sich auf Energieeffizienz, Lichtnutzung und Langzeitbeständigkeit konzentrieren, Schlüsselkonzepte in der Entwicklung unserer Projekte. Heutzutage ist Altamarea im Wohn- und Gewerbebereich tätig.

Altamarea est un bureau créé en 2015 par l'architecte Gonzalo Herreros et l'ingénieur Matias Quinlan, se distinguant principalement par le développement intégral de projets résidentiels et d'investissements pour la région côtière du Chili. L'architecture développée est en harmonie avec le lieu, reconnaissant les conditions climatiques et leurs variations tout au long de l'année. Les projets sont construits avec des matériaux simples d'origine locale, fournissant d'excellents résultats constructifs et architecturaux.
Forts de notre expérience de vie à la plage, nous créons des expériences de vie axées sur l'efficacité énergétique, l'utilisation optimale de la lumière et la durabilité, des concepts clés dans le développement de nos projets.

Altamarea es una oficina creada el año 2015 por el arquitecto Gonzalo Herreros y el ingeniero Matias Quinlan. Se ha caracterizado principalmente por el desarrollo integral de proyectos de vivienda e inversiones para la zona costera de Chile. Desarrollamos una arquitectura acorde al lugar reconociendo las condiciones climáticas y sus variables a lo largo del año. Construimos proyectos con materiales sencillos de origen local, con grandes resultados constructivos y arquitectónicos.
En base a nuestra experiencia de vida en la playa creamos para nuestros clientes experiencias de vida enfocados en la eficiencia energética, el aprovechamiento de la luz y la perdurabilidad en el tiempo, conceptos claves en el desarrollo de nuestro proyecto.

Concrete, wood, and iron converge in Altamarea's coastal home, merging architectural simplicity with the dynamic beauty of Chile's coastline.

Saint Étienne-du-Grès, Provence - Alpes-Côte d'Azur, France

LA FENIÈRE DANS LES ALPILLES MAISON

Experience the transformation of a traditional labyrinth into a light-filled Mediterranean retreat, where architectural artistry and natural materials evoke serenity and timeless design.

This dwelling was originally a labyrinth of small, dark rooms. Situated in a forest in the south of France, the architects saw its enormous potential and set about renovating it in the spirit of freedom and simplicity inherent in Mediterranean holiday homes. To gain space and natural light they re-organised the internal layout. They knocked down walls and relocated the rooms following a logical and fluid connection. They worked from a sculptural point of view so that curves, lines, objects, lights, passages and angles generated interesting compositions. In addition to the architectural solutions, this effect was also sought with the materials and colours. For the surfaces, they opted for Zellige terracotta tiles handmade in Morocco and Bejmat tiles, which allowed them to create a variety of patterns. The floor is also the result of natural and varnished Bejmats laid in a herringbone pattern. The wooden furniture and craftsman-inspired pieces stand out against the almost bare walls. To reinforce the flow, shelving and benches were used in selected areas of the house.

Cette demeure de était à l'origine un labyrinthe de petites pièces sombres. Située dans une forêt du sud de la France, les architectes ont vu son énorme potentiel et ont entrepris de la rénover dans l'esprit de liberté et de simplicité inhérent aux maisons de vacances méditerranéennes. Pour gagner de l'espace et de la lumière naturelle, ils ont réorganisé l'aménagement intérieur. Ils ont abattu des murs et déplacé les pièces en suivant une connexion logique et fluide. Ils ont travaillé d'un point de vue sculptural, de sorte que les courbes, les lignes, les objets, les lumières, les passages et les angles ont généré des compositions intéressantes. Outre les solutions architecturales, cet effet a également été recherché au niveau des matériaux et des couleurs. Pour les surfaces, ils ont opté pour des carreaux de terre cuite Zellige fabriqués à la main au Maroc et des carreaux Bejmat, ce qui leur a permis de créer une variété de motifs. Le sol est également le résultat de Bejmats naturels et vernis posés en chevrons. Les meubles en bois et les pièces d'inspiration artisanale se détachent sur les murs presque nus. Pour renforcer le flux, des étagères et des bancs ont été utilisés dans certaines zones de la maison.

Dieses Haus war ursprünglich ein Labyrinth aus kleinen, dunklen Räumen. In einem Wald in Südfrankreich gelegen, erkannten die Architekten das enorme Potenzial des Hauses und machten sich daran, es im Geiste der Freiheit und Schlichtheit der mediterranen Ferienhäuser zu renovieren. Um Platz und natürliches Licht zu gewinnen, wurde die Innenaufteilung neu organisiert. Sie rissen Wände ein und verlegten die Räume nach einer logischen und fließenden Verbindung. Sie arbeiteten nach bildhauerischen Gesichtspunkten, so dass Kurven, Linien, Objekte, Lichter, Durchgänge und Winkel interessante Kompositionen ergaben. Neben den architektonischen Lösungen wurde diese Wirkung auch mit den Materialien und Farben angestrebt. Für die Oberflächen entschieden sie sich für in Marokko handgefertigte Zellige-Terrakottafliesen und Bejmat-Fliesen, mit denen sie eine Vielzahl von Mustern gestalten konnten. Der Boden ist ebenfalls das Ergebnis von natürlichen und lackierten Bejmats, die in einem Fischgrätenmuster verlegt sind. Die Holzmöbel und handwerklich inspirierten Stücke heben sich von den fast kahlen Wänden ab. Um den Fluss zu verstärken, wurden in ausgewählten Bereichen des Hauses Regale und Bänke eingesetzt.

Esta vivienda era originalmente un laberinto de habitaciones pequeñas y oscuras. Situada en un bosque en el sur de Francia, los arquitectos vieron su enorme potencial y se plantearon reformarla con el espíritu de libertad y sencillez inherente a las casas de vacaciones mediterráneas. Para ganar espacio y luz natural reorganizaron la distribución interna. Derribaron muros y reubicaron las estancias siguiendo una conexión lógica y fluida. Se trabajó con un pnto de vista escultórico para que las curvas, las líneas, los objetos, las luces, los pasajes y los ángulos generen composiciones interesantes. Además de las soluciones arquitectónicas, se buscó ese efecto también con los materiales y las tonalidades. Para las superficies se decantaron por azulejos de terracota Zellige fabricados a mano en Marruecos, y baldosas Bejmat, que les permitieron crear variedad de patrones. El suelo también es resultado de un revestimiento a base de Bejmats naturales y barnizados colocados en forma de espiga. Los muebles de madera y las piezas de inspiración artesana resaltan frente a las paredes casi desnudas. Para reforzar la fluidez, se apostó por estanterías y bancos de obra en espacios seleccionados de la casa.

Photos: © Herve Hote

BOSC ARCHITECTES

Jean Bosc, Arthur Bosc

Forerunner of an experimental return to traditional techniques, architect Hugues Bosc, founded an agency in Saint Rémy in 1973, with a vision that has led to the revival of vernacular construction in French Provence. In 2013, Jean and Arthur Bosc took over the agency to create Bosc Architectes. Jean Bosc trained at the Julian ESAG Met Academy in Penninghen and at the Paris Belleville School of Architecture, and Arthur has a degree in engineering from the INP in Grenoble and graduated from the Ecole Nationale Supérieure d'Architecture in Marseille. Today, the management team is a duo that complements each other perfectly and exudes a joyful and creative energy.

Der Architekt Hugues Bosc, Vorreiter einer experimentellen Rückbesinnung auf traditionelle Techniken, gründete 1973 in Saint Rémy ein Büro mit einer Vision, die zu einer Wiederbelebung der traditionellen Bauweise in der französischen Provence führte. Im Jahr 2013 übernahmen Jean und Arthur Bosc das Büro und gründeten Bosc Architectes. Jean Bosc hat eine Ausbildung an der Julian ESAG Met Academy in Penninghen und an der Pariser Architekturschule Belleville absolviert, während Arthur einen Abschluss als Ingenieur am INP in Grenoble und einen Abschluss an der Ecole Nationale Supérieure d'Architecture in Marseille hat. Heute ist das Führungsteam ein Duo, das sich perfekt ergänzt und eine fröhliche und kreative Energie ausstrahlt.

Précurseur d'un retour expérimental aux techniques traditionnelles, l'architecte Hugues Bosc, a fondé une agence à Saint Rémy en 1973, avec une vision qui a conduit au renouveau de la construction vernaculaire en Provence française. En 2013, Jean et Arthur Bosc ont repris l'agence pour créer Bosc Architectes. Jean Bosc a été formé à l'Académie Julian ESAG Met de Penninghen et à l'école d'architecture de Paris Belleville. Arthur est ingénieur diplômé de l'INP de Grenoble et diplômé de l'Ecole Nationale Supérieure d'Architecture de Marseille. Aujourd'hui, l'équipe de direction est un duet qui se complète parfaitement et dégage une énergie joyeuse et créative.

Precursor de un retorno experimental a las técnicas tradicionales, el arquitecto Hugues Bosc, fundó una agencia en Saint Rémy en 1973, con una visión que ha propiciado el renacimiento de la construcción vernácula en la provenza francesa. En 2013, Jean y Arthur Bosc, retoman la agencia para crear Bosc Architectes. Jean Bosc se formó en la Academia Julian ESAG Met de Penninghen y en la Escuela de Arquitectura de París Belleville, y Arthur, es licenciado en ingeniería en el INP de Grenoble y graduado de la Escuela Nacional Superior de Arquitectura de Marsella. En la actualidad, el equipo directivo forma un dúo que se complementa perfectamente y desprende una gran energía alegre y creativa.

Curved lines and handcrafted Moroccan tiles merge harmoniously in this house, highlighting Bosc Architectes' talent for integrating tradition with contemporary aesthetics.

PROVENCE
ICONES
DE L'ART MODERNE
LA COLLECTION CHTCHOUKINE
FONDATION LOUIS VUITTON

THE GREEN APARTMENT

Natural light, custom furnishings, and artisanal materials transform The Green Apartment into a seamless blend of modern elegance and organic tranquility.

The Green Apartment is a private residence located in a luxury low density residential development in Singapore. The project consisted of an extensive renovation inspired by the lush gardens visible from the balcony.
There was a total reconfiguration of the apartment's layout for efficiency and an improved experience. In a newly designed entry foyer, a private lift vestibule opens into a dramatic gallery of sculptural green solid onyx pillars that act as a screen between the arrival space and the main common areas. In the living and dining rooms, textural richness continues and is seen on lightly silvered-stucco walls and ceilings, custom designed furniture and carpentry, all of which are paired with the adept curation of carefully sourced old and new pieces.
The indoor white oak flooring visually merges with the natural bleached teak floors at the balcony, where an existing sunken pool was levelled to increase the usable space of the terrace. On the balcony walls, terracotta tiles add depth and a traditional handcrafted touch.

The Green Apartment est une résidence privée située dans un lotissement de luxe à Singapour. Le projet consistait en une rénovation inspirée des jardins luxuriants visibles depuis le balcon.
L'agencement de l'appartement a été reconfiguré en faveur de l'efficacité et d'une expérience améliorée. Le nouveau hall d'entrée est un espace privé avec ascenseur qui s'ouvre sur une galerie spectaculaire de piliers en onyx vert massif, servant d'écran aux zones communes. Dans le salon et la salle à manger, la richesse des textures se retrouve dans les murs et les plafonds en stuc, les meubles sur mesure et les boiseries, le tout associé à une sélection de pièces anciennes et nouvelles. Le sol intérieur en chêne blanc s'harmonise visuellement avec le sol en teck blanchi naturel du balcon, où se trouve une piscine. Sur les murs du balcon, les carreaux en terre cuite ajoutent de la profondeur et une touche d'artisanat traditionnel.
Dans tout le reste de la maison, le bois de hickory occupe une place centrale. Associés à des tons neutres et à des tissus naturels dans les chambres, ils créent une atmosphère équilibrée et calme dans tous les espaces, qui dégagent une qualité masculine et zen.

The Green Apartment ist ein privates Wohnhaus in einer Luxuswohnanlage in Singapur. Das Projekt bestand aus einer Renovierung, die von den üppigen Gärten inspiriert war, die man vom Balkon aus sehen konnte.
Die neue Lobby ist ein privater Raum mit Aufzug, der sich zu einer dramatischen Galerie aus massiven grünen Onyxsäulen öffnet, die als Abschirmung zu den Gemeinschaftsbereichen dient. Im Wohn- und Esszimmer findet sich der Reichtum der Texturen in den Stuckwänden und -decken, den maßgefertigten Möbeln und Holzarbeiten, die mit einer Auswahl an antiken und neuen Stücken kombiniert sind. Der Innenboden aus weißer Eiche harmoniert optisch mit dem natürlichen, gebleichten Teakholzboden des Balkons, auf dem sich ein Swimmingpool befindet. An den Wänden des Balkons sorgen Terrakottafliesen für Tiefe und einen Hauch von traditioneller Handwerkskunst.
Im gesamten Haus steht das Hickoryholz im Mittelpunkt. In Kombination mit neutralen Tönen und natürlichen Stoffen in den Schlafzimmern wird eine ausgewogene und ruhige Atmosphäre in allen Räumen geschaffen, die eine maskuline, zenartige Qualität ausstrahlen.

The Green Apartment es una residencia privada en una urbanización de lujo en Singapur. El proyecto consistió en una renovación inspirada en los exuberantes jardines visibles desde el balcón.
El nuevo vestíbulo es un espacio privado con ascensor que se abre a una espectacular galería de pilares de ónice verde macizo, y que actúa como pantalla con las zonas comunes. En el salón y el comedor, la riqueza de texturas se aprecia en las paredes y los techos de estuco, los muebles a medida y la carpintería, todo ello combinado con una selección de piezas antiguas y nuevas. El suelo interior de roble blanco se funde visualmente con el suelo natural de teca blanqueada del balcón, donde se encuentra una piscina. En las paredes del balcón, las baldosas de terracota añaden profundidad y un toque artesanal tradicional.
En el resto de la casa, la madera de nogal americano es protagonista. Combinada con tonos neutros y tejidos naturales en los dormitorios, se consigue un ambiente equilibrado y tranquilo en todos los espacios, que desprenden una cualidad masculina y zen.

Photos: © Khoo Guo Jie

BREWIN DESIGN OFFICE

Robert Cheng

At Brewin Design Office, creativity is born of authenticity and affection, and is reflected in an artisanal approach to the creation of furniture and spaces, a perceptible passion for design and respect for the identity of each project. Working in different scales and genres has allowed for constant experimentation, with an overall ambition to achieve a sense of beauty governed by order, rhythm and detail. Since Robert Cheng founded the studio in 2012, this direction has remained steadfast. Cheng is an architect and interior designer. His philosophy is influenced by his knowledge and sensitivity to diverse cultures, the result of his extensive travels in Asia, America and Europe.

Bei Brewin Design Office entsteht Kreativität aus Authentizität und Zuneigung und spiegelt sich in einer handwerklichen Herangehensweise an die Gestaltung von Möbeln und Räumen, einer spürbaren Leidenschaft für Design und dem Respekt vor der Identität eines jeden Projekts wider. Die Arbeit in verschiedenen Maßstäben und Genres ermöglichte ein ständiges Experimentieren mit dem Ziel, einen Sinn für Schönheit zu erreichen, der von Ordnung, Rhythmus und Details bestimmt wird. Seit der Gründung des Studios durch Robert Cheng im Jahr 2012 ist diese Richtung ungebrochen. Cheng ist Architekt und Innenarchitekt. Seine Philosophie ist geprägt von seinem Wissen und seiner Sensibilität für verschiedene Kulturen, die er auf seinen ausgedehnten Reisen in Asien, Amerika und Europa erworben hat.

Chez Brewin Design Office, la créativité naît de l'authenticité et de l'affection, et se traduit par une approche artisanale de la création de meubles et d'espaces, une passion perceptible pour le design et le respect de l'identité de chaque projet. Travailler à différentes échelles et dans différents genres a permis une expérimentation constante, avec l'ambition générale d'atteindre un sens de la beauté régi par l'ordre, le rythme et le détail. Depuis que Robert Cheng a fondé le studio en 2012, cette orientation est restée inébranlable. Cheng est architecte et décorateur d'intérieur. Sa philosophie est influencée par ses connaissances et sa sensibilité à l'égard de diverses cultures, fruit de ses nombreux voyages en Asie, en Amérique et en Europe.

En Brewin Design Office, la creatividad nace de la autenticidad y el afecto, y se refleja en un enfoque artesanal hacia la creación de muebles y espacios, una pasión perceptible por el diseño y el respeto por la identidad de cada proyecto. Trabajar a distintas escalas y géneros le ha permitido una experimentación constante, con la ambición general de alcanzar una sensación de belleza regida por el orden, el ritmo y el detalle. Desde que Robert Cheng fundó el estudio en 2012, esta dirección se ha mantenido firme. Cheng es arquitecto y diseñador de interiores. Su filosofía está influenciada por sus conocimientos y sensibilidades hacia diversas culturas, fruto de sus extensos viajes por Asia, América y Europa.

Almières, La Lozère, France

LE PAVILLON

This serene pavilion seamlessly merges traditional materials and modern design, offering a warm, minimalist retreat in harmony with the dramatic Tarn Gorges.

This contemporary design pavilion, which seems to be suspended over the breathtaking Tarn Gorges, is the refuge that the couple commissioned the owners to build to escape from the city and live in a calm and serene environment, close to their venture project, the Almières Retreat, where they organise yoga and wellness retreats. To reinforce this feeling, the choice of materials was key. On the outside, the combination of local wood in the latticework and stone on the walls blends in with the rocky mountain. Inside, natural oak wood in different finishes covers the ceilings, floors and walls, creating an extension of the interior to the exterior. The designer combined traditional materials such as black zimbawe granite in the kitchen with natural textures such as linen and wool in the curtains, creating an elegant atmosphere of warmth and comfort, even in sub-zero temperatures in winter, thanks to the suspended fireplace in the living room. Simplicity in the design of the spaces and furnishings, as well as carefully considered lighting, contribute to creating a minimalist and calm interior, "a haven for the soul."

Ce pavillon au design contemporain, qui semble suspendu au-dessus des époustouflantes Gorges du Tarn, est le refuge que le couple a fait construire pour s'échapper de la ville et vivre dans un environnement calme et serein, à proximité de leur projet d'entreprise, la Retraite des Almières, où ils organisent des retraites de yoga et de bien-être. Pour renforcer ce sentiment, le choix des matériaux était essentiel. À l'extérieur, la combinaison de bois local dans les treillis et de pierre sur les murs s'harmonise avec la montagne rocheuse. À l'intérieur, du bois de chêne naturel de différentes finitions recouvre les plafonds, les sols et les murs, créant ainsi une extension de l'intérieur vers l'extérieur. Le designer a combiné des matériaux traditionnels tels que le granit noir zimbawe dans la cuisine avec des textures naturelles comme le lin et la laine dans les rideaux, créant ainsi une atmosphère élégante, chaleureuse et confortable, même par des températures négatives en hiver, grâce à la cheminée suspendue dans le salon. La simplicité de la conception des espaces et du mobilier, ainsi qu'un éclairage soigneusement étudié, contribuent à créer un intérieur minimaliste et calme, « un havre pour l'âme ».

Dieser zeitgenössische Design-Pavillon, der über der atemberaubenden Gorges du Tarn zu schweben scheint, ist das Refugium, das das Ehepaar den Eigentümern in Auftrag gegeben hat, um der Stadt zu entfliehen und in einer ruhigen und gelassenen Umgebung zu leben, in der Nähe ihres Projekts, dem Almières Retreat, wo sie Yoga- und Wellness-Retreats veranstalten. Um dieses Gefühl zu verstärken, war die Wahl der Materialien entscheidend. Von außen fügt sich die Kombination aus einheimischem Holz im Fachwerk und Stein an den Wänden in die felsige Bergwelt ein. Im Inneren sind Decken, Böden und Wände mit natürlichem Eichenholz in verschiedenen Ausführungen verkleidet, so dass sich der Innenraum nach außen hin verlängert. Der Designer kombinierte traditionelle Materialien wie schwarzen Zimbawe-Granit in der Küche mit natürlichen Texturen wie Leinen und Wolle in den Vorhängen und schuf so eine elegante Atmosphäre der Wärme und Behaglichkeit, selbst bei Minusgraden im Winter, dank des hängenden Kamins im Wohnzimmer. Die schlichte Gestaltung der Räume und des Mobiliars sowie die durchdachte Beleuchtung tragen dazu bei, ein minimalistisches und ruhiges Interieur zu schaffen, „eine Oase für die Seele."

Éste pabellón de diseño contemporáneo que parece estar suspendido sobre las impresionantes Gargantas del Tarn, es el refugio que encargaron construir la pareja de propietarias para huir de la ciudad y vivir en un entorno de calma y serenidad, cerca de su proyecto de emprendimiento, el Almières Retreat, donde organizan retiros de yoga y bienestar. Para reforzar ese sentimiento, la selección de los materiales fue clave. En el exterior la combinación de la madera autóctona en las celosías y la piedra en las paredes se confunden con la montaña rocosa. En el interior, la madera de roble natural en distintos acabados, reviste techos, suelos y paredes, creando una prolongación del interior hacía el exterior. La diseñadora combinó materiales tradicionales como el granito negro zimbawe en la cocina, con texturas naturales como el lino, o la lana en las cortinas, creando una atmósfera elegante de calidez y confort, incluso con temperaturas bajo cero en el invierno, gracias a la chimenea suspendida en el salón. La simplicidad en el diseño de los espacios y del mobiliario, así como una estudiada iluminación contribuye a crear un interior minimalista y calmo, «un refugio para el alma».

Photos: © Eugeni Pons

CARME PARDO ARQUITECTURA INTERIOR

Carme Pardo

Carme Pardo trained at the Escuela Superior de Diseño de Interiores EIADE in Barcelona. After creating her first studio specialising in textiles, where she discovered the importance of textures and working with natural and neutral materials, she began her professional career in 2008. As an interior designer she has carried out projects in Spain and the south of France. Her works are mainly residential, although in recent years she has also ventured into the field of small charming hotels. "I like functional interiors without excesses, which form part of the context and the architecture, working with shapes and light, explains the designer. We seek to create balanced and timeless spaces, tailor-made suits for each client."

Carme Pardo absolvierte ihre Ausbildung an der Escuela Superior de Diseño de Interiores EIADE in Barcelona. Nach der Gründung ihres ersten auf Textilien spezialisierten Studios, in dem sie die Bedeutung von Texturen und die Arbeit mit natürlichen und neutralen Materialien entdeckte, begann sie 2008 ihre berufliche Laufbahn. Als Innenarchitektin hat sie Projekte in Spanien und Südfrankreich verwirklicht. Ihre Arbeiten sind vor allem im Wohnbereich angesiedelt, obwohl sie sich in den letzten Jahren auch in den Bereich der kleinen charmanten Hotels vorgewagt hat. „Ich mag funktionale Innenräume ohne Übertreibungen, die sich in den Kontext und die Architektur einfügen und mit Formen und Licht arbeiten, erklärt der Designer, wir versuchen, ausgewogene und zeitlose Räume zu schaffen, die für jeden Kunden maßgeschneidert sind."

Carme Pardo a suivi une formation à l'Escuela Superior de Diseño de Interiores EIADE de Barcelone. Après avoir créé son premier atelier spécialisé dans le textile, où elle a découvert l'importance des textures et du travail avec des matériaux naturels et neutres, elle a commencé sa carrière professionnelle en 2008. En tant qu'architecte d'intérieur, elle a réalisé des projets en Espagne et dans le sud de la France. Ses travaux sont principalement résidentiels, bien que ces dernières années, elle se soit également aventurée dans le domaine des petits hôtels de charme. « J'aime les intérieurs fonctionnels sans excès, qui s'intègrent au contexte et à l'architecture, en travaillant les formes et la lumière, explique le designer. Nous cherchons à créer des espaces équilibrés et intemporels, des costumes sur mesure pour chaque client ».

Carme Pardo se formó en la Escuela Superior de Diseño de Interiores EIADE de Barcelona. Después de crear su primer estudio especializado en textiles, donde descubrió la importancia de las texturas y de trabajar con materiales naturales y neutros, en 2008 inició su trayectoria profesional. Como diseñadora de interiores ha realizado proyectos en España y el sur de Francia. Sus trabajos son principalmente residenciales, aunque en los últimos años también ha incursionado en el campo de los pequeños hoteles con encanto. «Me gustan los interiores funcionales y sin excesos, que formen parte del contexto y de la arquitectura, trabajando con las formas y la luz —explica la diseñadora— Buscamos crear espacios equilibrados y atemporales, trajes a medida para cada cliente».

CHAMANES

SKY GARDEN

Natural timbers and serene tones infuse Sky Garden's interiors with a warmth and sophistication that complements its striking architectural design.

CLO Studios provided the interior decoration for this project by building designers Chris Clout Design, located in the exclusive area of Noosa Queensland. Taking a counterpoint to the home's very defined exteriors, a neutral and soothing palette was created for the interiors. With the use of natural Australian timbers, and the choice of serene colours taken from the environment, the house gained warmth. A detail that is unique to this house was applied to each space in Sky Garden, such as the custom-designed furniture. The 4.5 m long dining table is made from blackbutt wood, with logs hand milled by a local craftsman. At the entrance, a stunning 3D artwork commissioned from local artist Stacy Madden (Woven Husk) stands out. The piece is paired with a cowhide rug by Kyle Bunting. The pool area represents the owners' desire for a colourful and fun area. The key was to create a space that was not distinct from the interior, but an extension of the design with a playful twist.

CLO Studios a assuré la décoration intérieure de ce projet des desinateurs de bâtiments Chris Clout Design, situé dans la zone exclusive de Noosa Queensland. En contrepoint des extérieurs très définis de la maison, une palette neutre et apaisante a été créée pour les intérieurs. Avec l'utilisation de bois naturel australien et le choix de couleurs sereines tirées de l'environnement, la maison a gagné en chaleur. Un détail qui est unique à cette maison a été appliqué à chaque espace de Sky Garden, comme le mobilier conçu sur mesure. La table à manger de 4,5 m de long est fabriquée en bois de blackbutt, dont les rondins sont fraisés à la main par un artisan local. À l'entrée, une étonnante œuvre d'art en 3D commandée à l'artiste locale Stacy Madden (Woven Husk) se détache. La pièce est associée à un tapis en peau de vache de Kyle Bunting. L'espace piscine représente le désir des propriétaires d'avoir un espace coloré et amusant. La clé était de créer un espace qui ne soit pas distinct de l'intérieur, mais une extension du design avec une touche ludique.

CLO Studios lieferte das Innendesign für dieses Projekt des bauplaner Chris Clout Design, das in der exklusiven Gegend von Noosa Queensland liegt. Als Kontrapunkt zu den scharf umrissenen Außenbereichen des Hauses wurde für die Innenräume eine neutrale und beruhigende Farbpalette geschaffen. Durch die Verwendung natürlicher australischer Hölzer und die Wahl ruhiger, der Umgebung entnommener Farben erhielt das Haus eine warme Ausstrahlung. Ein für dieses Haus einzigartiges Detail wurde in jedem Raum von Sky Garden angewandt, wie z. B. die speziell entworfenen Möbel. Der 4,5 m lange Esstisch ist aus Schwarzbutt-Holz gefertigt, dessen Stämme von einem örtlichen Handwerker handgefräst wurden. Am Eingang sticht ein beeindruckendes 3D-Kunstwerk ins Auge, das bei der lokalen Künstlerin Stacy Madden (Woven Husk) in Auftrag gegeben wurde. Das Stück wird mit einem Kuhfellteppich von Kyle Bunting kombiniert. Der Poolbereich entspricht dem Wunsch der Eigentümer nach einem farbenfrohen und unterhaltsamen Bereich. Der Schlüssel war, einen Raum zu schaffen, der sich nicht von der Inneneinrichtung unterscheidet, sondern eine Erweiterung des Designs mit einer spielerischen Note ist.

CLO Studios se encargó de la decoración en este proyecto de los proyectistas Chris Clout Design, situado en la exclusiva zona de Noosa Queensland. Tomando como contrapunto los exteriores muy definidos de la vivienda, se creó una paleta neutra y relajante para los interiores. Con el uso de maderas naturales australianas, y la elección de colores serenos tomados del entorno, la casa ganó calidez. En cada espacio de Sky Garden se aplicó un detalle que es exclusivo para esta casa, como los muebles diseñados a medida. La mesa del comedor de 4,5 metros de largo está hecha con madera de blackbutt, y troncos fresados a mano por un artesano local. En la entrada, destaca una impresionante obra de arte en 3D encargada al artista local Stacy Madden (Woven Husk). La pieza combina con una alfombra de piel de vaca de Kyle Bunting. El área de la piscina representa la voluntad de los propietarios de contar con una zona colorida y divertida. La clave era crear un espacio que no se diferenciara del interior, sino que fuera una extensión del diseño con un toque lúdico.

Photos: © David Chatfield

CLO STUDIOS

Chloe Tozer

CLO Studios was conceived by mother and daughter designers Trudy and Chloe Tozer. Combining Trudy's extensive interior design experience, and Chloe's established background in Fine Art and Jewellery, a multi-disciplinary partnership was forged between the two. Chloe's innate curiosity and fearless, intuitive approach to design is the foundation of the firm. Inspiration is drawn from the world's rich and vibrant cultures, from which she weaves her artistic narratives with each client's desires. Her aim is to create spaces to be admired through work that is based on research and careful design resulting in luxury residential interiors and bespoke commercial spaces.

CLO Studios wurde von den Designerinnen Trudy und Chloe Tozer, Mutter und Tochter, gegründet. Durch die Kombination von Trudys umfassender Erfahrung in der Innenarchitektur und Chloes fundiertem Hintergrund in den Bereichen Kunst und Schmuck wurde eine multidisziplinäre Partnerschaft zwischen den beiden geschmiedet. Chloes angeborene Neugier und ihre furchtlose, intuitive Herangehensweise an das Design sind die Grundlage des Unternehmens. Ihre Inspiration schöpft sie aus den reichen und lebendigen Kulturen der Welt, aus denen sie ihre künstlerischen Erzählungen mit den Wünschen ihrer Kunden verwebt. Ihr Ziel ist es, durch ihre Arbeit, die auf Forschung und sorgfältigem Design basiert, Räume zu schaffen, die bewundert werden können, und so luxuriöse Wohnräume und maßgeschneiderte Geschäftsräume zu schaffen.

CLO Studios a été conçu par les designers mère et fille Trudy et Chloe Tozer. En combinant la vaste expérience de Trudy dans le domaine de la décoration d'intérieur et l'expérience de Chloé dans le domaine des beaux-arts et de la bijouterie, un partenariat multidisciplinaire s'est formé entre les deux. La curiosité innée de Chloé et son approche intrépide et intuitive du design constituent le fondement de l'entreprise. Elle puise son inspiration dans les cultures riches et vibrantes du monde, à partir desquelles elle tisse ses récits artistiques en fonction des désirs de chaque client. Son objectif est de créer des espaces qui suscitent l'admiration grâce à un travail basé sur la recherche et une conception soignée, qui se traduit par des intérieurs résidentiels de luxe et des espaces commerciaux sur mesure.

CLO Studios fue concebido por las diseñadoras Trudy y Chloe Tozer, madre e hija. Combinando la amplia experiencia en diseño de interiores de Trudy, y la consolidada formación de Chloe en Bellas Artes y Joyería, se forjó una asociación multidisciplinar entre ambas. La curiosidad innata y el enfoque valiente e intuitivo de Chloe hacia el diseño son la base de la firma. La inspiración son las diferentes culturas del mundo, ricas y vibrantes, de las cuales entrelaza sus narrativas artísticas con los deseos de cada cliente. Su objetivo es crear espacios para ser admirados y su trabajo, se basa en la investigación en profundidad y el diseño cuidadoso que resulta en interiores residenciales de lujo y comerciales a medida.

Custom furniture and locally sourced artistry highlight CLO Studios' ability to blend luxury and creativity in every detail.

CASA AVIV

A serene refuge in the Tulum jungle, Casa Aviv seamlessly blends minimalism and natural materials, creating an airy, tranquil environment deeply connected to nature.

Just a stone's throw from Tulum beach and crystal-clear cenotes, this house hides discreetly in the jungle, opening to the outside to create a haven of tranquillity. Composed of two parallel volumes, the house has four en-suite bedrooms, all with views of the jungle. The master bedroom has direct access to the swimming pool and private patio. The living-dining room and kitchen share a double-height space that extends out to the pool and garden through the floor-to-ceiling pivoting glass doors. The result is an integrated environment, full of natural light and visually connected to the garden. The house is oriented from east to west, taking advantage of the winds coming from the coast to achieve cross ventilation. The finishes and materials used have been handcrafted. The warm grey polished cement walls contrast with the black terrazzo floors. Charred cedar woodwork complements a neutral colour palette. Furniture and light fittings were custom-designed and sourced or manufactured locally. The solid appearance of the house reflects the durability and low maintenance needs of a rental property in a tropical climate.

Nur einen Steinwurf vom Strand von Tulum und den kristallklaren Cenoten entfernt, versteckt sich dieses Haus diskret im Dschungel und öffnet sich nach außen, um eine Oase der Ruhe zu schaffen. Das Haus besteht aus zwei parallelen Volumen und hat vier Schlafzimmer mit eigenem Bad, alle mit Blick auf den Dschungel. Das Wohn-Esszimmer und die Küche teilen sich einen Raum mit doppelter Höhe, der sich durch die bodentiefen Glasschwingtüren zum Pool und Garten hin öffnet. Das Ergebnis ist eine integrierte Umgebung voller natürlichem Licht und mit einer visuellen Verbindung zum Garten. Das Haus ist von Osten nach Westen ausgerichtet, um die von der Küste kommenden Winde für eine Querlüftung zu nutzen. Die verwendeten Oberflächen und Materialien sind handgefertigt. Die warmen grauen, polierten Zementwände stehen im Kontrast zu den schwarzen Terrazzoböden. Gekohlte Zedernholzarbeiten ergänzen eine neutrale Farbpalette. Möbel und Beleuchtungskörper wurden individuell entworfen und vor Ort beschafft oder hergestellt. Das solide Erscheinungsbild des Hauses spiegelt die Langlebigkeit und den geringen Wartungsbedarf eines Mietobjekts in einem tropischen Klima wider.

À deux pas de la plage de Tulum et des cénotes aux eaux cristallines, cette maison se cache discrètement dans la jungle, s'ouvrant sur l'extérieur pour créer un havre de tranquillité. Composée de deux volumes parallèles, la maison dispose de quatre chambres en-suite, toutes avec vue sur la jungle. La chambre principale a un accès direct à la piscine et au patio privé. Le salon-salle à manger et la cuisine partagent un espace à double hauteur qui s'étend vers la piscine et le jardin à travers les portes vitrées pivotantes du sol au plafond. Le résultat est un environnement intégré, plein de lumière naturelle et visuellement connecté au jardin. La maison est orientée d'est en ouest, profitant des vents venant de la côte pour obtenir une ventilation croisée. Les finitions et les matériaux utilisés ont été réalisés de manière artisanale. Les murs en ciment poli gris chaud contrastent avec les sols en terrazzo noir. Les boiseries en cèdre carbonisé complètent une palette de couleurs neutres. Les meubles et les luminaires ont été conçus sur mesure et achetés ou fabriqués localement. L'apparence solide de la maison reflète la durabilité et les besoins d'entretien réduits d'une propriété locative dans un climat tropical.

A tan solo un paso de la playa de Tulum y de los cristalinos cenotes, esta casa se esconde discretamente en la jungla, abriéndose al exterior para crear un reductos de tranquilidad. Compuesta por dos volúmenes paralelos, la vivienda cuenta con cuatro habitaciones, todas con vistas a la jungla, y baño. La sala-comedor y cocina comparten un espacio a doble altura que se extiende hacia la piscina y el jardín a través de las puertas de vidrio pivotantes, de piso a techo. Como resultado se genera un ambiente integrado, lleno de luz natural y conectado visualmente al jardín. La casa está orientada de este a oeste, aprovechando los vientos que llegan desde la costa para lograr así una ventilación cruzada. Los acabados y materiales utilizados han sido producidos artesanalmente. Los muros de cemento pulido gris cálido, contrastan con los suelos de terrazzo negro. La carpintería en madera de cedro carbonizada complementa la paleta neutra. Los muebles y luminarias se diseñaron a medida y se obtuvieron o fabricaron localmente. Eel aspecto solido de la casa refleja las necesidades de durabilidad y bajo mantenimiento de una propiedad de alquiler en un clima tropical.

Photos: © César Bejar

CO-LAB DESIGN OFFICE

Joana Gomes, Joshua Beck

Founded by Joana Gomes and Joshua Beck in 2010, CO-LAB DESIGN OFFICE is an architecture, design and construction studio based in Tulum, Mexico. Inspired by the natural beauty of Yucatan, their projects foster a deep connection with the natural world. Their work embraces sustainable principles, prioritising the use of locally sourced natural materials and handcrafted finishes. The aesthetic tends towards a certain raw minimalism mitigated by the use of landscaping and organic, handcrafted finishes. The office is part design studio and part workshop where objects, furniture and accessories are prototyped, and techniques and materials are experimented with.

Das 2010 von Joana Gomes und Joshua Beck gegründete CO-LAB DESIGN OFFICE ist ein Architektur-, Design- und Konstruktionsbüro mit Sitz in Tulum, Mexiko. Inspiriert von der natürlichen Schönheit Yucatans, fördern ihre Projekte eine tiefe Verbundenheit mit der natürlichen Welt. Sie arbeiten nach nachhaltigen Grundsätzen und verwenden vorrangig natürliche Materialien aus der Region und handgefertigte Oberflächen. Die Ästhetik tendiert zu einem gewissen rohen Minimalismus, der durch die Verwendung von Landschaftsgestaltung und organischen, handgefertigten Oberflächen gemildert wird. Das Büro ist zum Teil Designstudio und zum Teil Werkstatt, in der Objekte, Möbel und Accessoires als Prototypen entwickelt und mit Techniken und Materialien experimentiert wird.

Fondé par Joana Gomes et Joshua Beck en 2010, CO-LAB DESIGN OFFICE est un studio d'architecture, de design et de construction basé à Tulum, au Mexique. Inspirés par la beauté naturelle du Yucatan, leurs projets favorisent un lien profond avec le monde naturel. Leur travail s'appuie sur des principes durables, privilégiant l'utilisation de matériaux naturels d'origine locale et de finitions artisanales. L'esthétique tend vers un certain minimalisme brut atténué par l'utilisation de l'aménagement paysager et de finitions organiques et artisanales. Le bureau est à la fois un studio de design et un atelier où des objets, des meubles et des accessoires sont prototypés, et où des techniques et des matériaux sont expérimentés.

Fundado por Joana Gomes y Joshua Beck en 2010, CO-LAB DESIGN OFFICE es un estudio de arquitectura, diseño y construcción con sede en Tulum, México. Inspirados en la belleza natural de Yucatán, sus proyectos fomentan una profunda conexión con el mundo natural. Su trabajo adopta principios sostenibles, prioriza el uso de materiales naturales de origen local y los acabados artesanales. La estética tiende hacia cierto minimalismo crudo mitigado por el uso del paisajismo y los acabados orgánicos y artesanales. La oficina es parte estudio de diseño y parte taller en el que se prototipan objetos, muebles y accesorios, y se experimenta con técnicas y materiales.

Handcrafted materials, charred cedar, and polished cement unite in Casa Aviv, showcasing CO-LAB DESIGN OFFICE's commitment to sustainable design and harmonious living.

OSTERIA BETULLA

A modern Italian canteen, Osteria Betulla blends classic references with minimalist elegance, creating a serene space where simple, high-quality cuisine takes center stage.

Osteria Betulla is a restaurant by the talented chef, Arslan Berdi. The gastronomic proposal is Italian cuisine, simple and with very high quality products. The design concept of the space is that of a modern Italian canteen with references to the classic. The image resembles an uncluttered, light-filled chapel. The furnishings refer to Catholic aesthetics. The centre piece of the first room is a metaphorical altar: a large work table for the cook who is in charge of the pasta, with all the tables turned towards him. The highlight of the second room are the church pews in the centre and three icon boxes with the Holy Trinity of Italian cuisine: wine, olive oil and thyme. The drinking troughs common in Italian cities take the form of a wine cooler in the living room and a sink in the bathrooms. The designers' aim was to create a very clean and minimalist look, with as little expressiveness as possible. That is why they used only three basic materials: travertine marble, which is often found in Italian street pavements; wood for the furniture and panelling; and light-coloured plaster as the main material for the walls.

Osteria Betulla est un restaurant du talentueux chef Arslan Berdi. La proposition gastronomique est une cuisine italienne, simple et avec des produits de très haute qualité. Le concept de l'espace est celui d'une cantine italienne moderne avec des références au classique. L'image ressemble à une chapelle épurée et lumineuse. L'ameublement fait référence à l'esthétique catholique. La pièce maîtresse de la première salle est un autel métaphorique : une grande table de travail pour le cuisinier qui s'occupe des pâtes, avec toutes les tables tournées vers lui. Le clou de la deuxième pièce est constitué par les bancs d'église au centre et trois boîtes d'icônes avec la Sainte Trinité de la cuisine italienne : vin, huile d'olive et thym. Les abreuvoirs courants dans les villes italiennes prennent la forme d'un refroidisseur de vin dans le salon et d'un évier dans les salles de bains. L'objectif des concepteurs était de créer un look très épuré et minimaliste, avec le moins d'expressivité possible. Ils n'ont donc utilisé que trois matériaux de base : le marbre travertin, que l'on trouve couramment sur les trottoirs italiens, le bois pour les meubles et les lambris, et le plâtre clair comme matériau principal des murs.

Osteria Betulla ist ein Restaurant des talentierten Küchenchefs Arslan Berdi. Das gastronomische Angebot ist italienische Küche, einfach und mit sehr hochwertigen Produkten. Das Designkonzept des Raums ist das einer modernen italienischen Kantine mit Bezügen zur Klassik. Das Bild ähnelt einer unaufgeräumten, lichtdurchfluteten Kapelle. Das Mobiliar verweist auf die katholische Ästhetik. Das Herzstück des ersten Raums ist ein metaphorischer Altar: ein großer Arbeitstisch für den Koch, der für die Pasta zuständig ist, und alle Tische sind ihm zugewandt. Das Highlight des zweiten Raums sind die Kirchenbänke in der Mitte und drei Ikonenkästen mit der Heiligen Dreifaltigkeit der italienischen Küche: Wein, Olivenöl und Thymian. Die in italienischen Städten üblichen Tränken haben die Form eines Weinkühlers im Wohnzimmer und eines Waschbeckens in den Badezimmern. Das Ziel der Designer war es, ein sehr klares und minimalistisches Aussehen zu schaffen, mit so wenig Ausdrucksmöglichkeiten wie möglich. Deshalb wurden nur drei grundlegende Materialien verwendet: Travertinmarmor, der häufig in italienischen Straßenpflastern zu finden ist, Holz für die Möbel und die Vertäfelung sowie heller Putz als Hauptmaterial für die Wände.

Osteria Betulla es un restaurante del talentoso chef, Arslan Berdi. La propuesta gastronómica es de cocina italiana, sencilla y con productos de muy alta calidad. El concepto de diseño del espacio, es el de una cantina italiana moderna con referencias a lo clásico. La imagen se asemeja a una capilla despejada y llena de luz. El mobiliario hace referencia a la estética católica. La pieza central de la primera sala es un altar metafórico: una gran mesa de trabajo para el cocinero que se encarga de la pasta, con todas las mesas giradas hacia él. El punto fuerte de la segunda sala son los bancos de iglesia en el centro y tres cajas de iconos con la Santísima Trinidad de la cocina italiana: el vino, el aceite de oliva y el tomillo. Los bebederos habituales en las ciudades italianas por su parte, adoptaron la forma de enfriador de vino en la sala, y de lavabo en los baños. El objetivo de los diseñadores fue crear un aspecto muy pulcro y minimalista, con la menor expresividad posible. Por eso utilizaron solo tres materiales básicos: el travertino, que suele encontrarse en los pavimentos de las calles italianas; madera para los muebles y paneles, y yeso de color claro como material principal en las paredes.

Photos: © Sergey Melnikov

DA BUREAU

Boris Lvovsky, Anna Lvovskaya, Fedor Goreglyad, Maria Romanova

Da Bureau is a team of young architects based in St. Petersburg and Tallinn with the motto "we create interior architecture." The firm has won a number of international awards, including the "Rising Star" award for its founder Boris Lvovsky in Interior Design Magazine's Best of Year in the United States. It has also been on AD Russia magazine's list of the top 100 designers and architects and among the five finalists of the Architizer A+ Awards in the young interior design firm category. He regularly participates in the British Restaurant and Bar Design Awards. His projects are identified by a contemporary, minimalist style and a functionality-oriented approach.

Da Bureau ist ein Team junger Architekten mit Sitz in St. Petersburg und Tallinn und dem Motto „Wir schaffen Innenarchitektur." Das Unternehmen hat eine Reihe von internationalen Auszeichnungen erhalten, darunter die Auszeichnung „Rising Star" für seinen Gründer Boris Lvovsky im Rahmen des Interior Design Magazine's Best of Year in den Vereinigten Staaten. Darüber hinaus wurde es von der Zeitschrift AD Russia in die Liste der 100 besten Designer und Architekten aufgenommen und gehörte zu den fünf Finalisten der Architizer A+ Awards in der Kategorie junge Innenarchitekturbüros. Er nimmt regelmäßig an den British Restaurant and Bar Design Awards teil. Seine Projekte zeichnen sich durch einen zeitgenössischen, minimalistischen Stil und einen funktionsorientierten Ansatz aus.

Da Bureau est une équipe de jeunes architectes basée à Saint-Pétersbourg et à Tallinn qui adopte la devise « nous créons de l'architecture intérieure ». Le cabinet a remporté un certain nombre de prix internationaux, notamment le prix « Rising Star » pour son fondateur Boris Lvovsky dans le cadre du concours « Best of Year » de l'Interior Design Magazine aux États-Unis. Elle a également figuré sur la liste des 100 meilleurs designers et architectes du magazine AD Russia et parmi les cinq finalistes des Architizer A+ Awards dans la catégorie des jeunes entreprises de design d'intérieur. Il participe régulièrement aux British Restaurant and Bar Design Awards. Ses projets se caractérisent par un style contemporain et minimaliste et une approche axée sur la fonctionnalité.

Da Bureau es un equipo de jóvenes arquitectos con sede en San Petersburgo y Tallin que se acoge al lema «creamos arquitectura interior». La firma cuenta con un gran número de galardones internacionales, entre ellos el de «Estrella Emergente» de su fundador Boris Lvovsky, en el Best of Year de Interior Design Magazine, en Estados Unidos. También ha estado en la lista de los 100 mejores diseñadores y arquitectos de la revista AD Russia y entre los cinco finalistas de Architizer A+ Awards en la categoría de firma joven de interiorismo. Participa regularmente en los British Restaurant and Bar Design Awards. Sus proyectos se caracterizan por un estilo contemporáneo y minimalista, y un enfoque orientado a la funcionalidad.

Travertine marble, wood paneling, and a central "altar" reflect Da Bureau's contemporary take on Italian canteen design, balancing functionality and tradition.

LLAFRANC

Natural tones, Mediterranean materials, and thoughtful spatial divisions transform this Costa Brava home into a serene retreat for a modern family.

The design of this new-build house on the Costa Brava responds to the request of a family looking for a country and beach house that would allow them to disconnect from the hectic pace of modern life. The contemporary architecture of the building by architect Damián Ribas was the canvas on which Clara Joly d'Aussy set out to give the house warmth by bringing the Mediterranean and the greenery of the Empordà into the interior. To achieve this, she used wood in furniture and cladding, natural fibers such as rattan, jute and esparto grass, and beige and earth tones. One of the biggest challenges was to separate the kitchen, dining room and living room. To filter the light and divide these spaces without closing them off, the interior designer used vertical sliding doors made of wooden slats. The same slats, but horizontally, complete the cupboards and interior doors, giving the house continuity. The lighting has been another key aesthetic element: industrial lamps mixed with rattan and other paper lamps create a warm atmosphere which, combined with the wood, create a spirit of pure holiday relaxation.

La conception de cette maison de construction neuve sur la Costa Brava répond à la demande d'une famille qui recherchait une maison de campagne et de plage qui leur permettrait de se déconnecter du rythme effréné de la vie moderne. L'architecture contemporaine du bâtiment de l'architecte Damian Ribas a été la toile sur laquelle Clara Joly d'Aussy a entrepris de donner de la chaleur à la maison en faisant entrer la Méditerranée et la verdure de l'Empordà à l'intérieur. Pour ce faire, elle a utilisé le bois dans les meubles et les revêtements, des fibres naturelles telles que le rotin, le jute et l'alfa, ainsi que des tons beiges et terreux. L'un des plus grands défis était de séparer la cuisine, la salle à manger et le salon. Pour filtrer la lumière et diviser ces espaces sans les fermer, l'architecte d'intérieur a utilisé des portes coulissantes verticales en lattes de bois. Les mêmes lattes, mais horizontalement, complètent les armoires et les portes intérieures, donnant ainsi une continuité à la maison. L'éclairage a été un autre élément esthétique clé : les lampes industrielles mélangées au rotin et autres lampes en papier créent une atmosphère chaleureuse qui, associée au bois, crée un esprit de pure détente de vacances.

Der Entwurf dieses Neubaus an der Costa Brava entspricht dem Wunsch einer Familie, die ein Haus auf dem Land und am Strand suchte, um von der Hektik des modernen Lebens abschalten zu können. Die zeitgenössische Architektur des Gebäudes des Architekten Damián Ribas war die Leinwand, auf der Clara Joly d'Aussy dem Haus Wärme verleihen wollte, indem sie das Mittelmeer und das Grün des Empordà in das Innere brachte. Um dies zu erreichen, verwendete sie Holz für Möbel und Verkleidungen, Naturfasern wie Rattan, Jute und Espartogras sowie Beige- und Erdtöne. Eine der größten Herausforderungen bestand darin, Küche, Esszimmer und Wohnzimmer voneinander zu trennen. Um das Licht zu filtern und die Räume zu unterteilen, ohne sie zu verschließen, verwendete der Innenarchitekt vertikale Schiebetüren aus Holzlamellen. Die gleichen Latten, jedoch horizontal, vervollständigen die Schränke und Innentüren und verleihen dem Haus Kontinuität. Die Beleuchtung ist ein weiteres ästhetisches Schlüsselelement: Industrielampen, gemischt mit Rattan- und anderen Papierlampen, schaffen eine warme Atmosphäre, die in Verbindung mit dem Holz ein Gefühl von purer Urlaubsentspannung erzeugt.

El diseño de esta casa de obra nueva en la Costa Brava responde al requerimiento de una familia que buscaba una casa de campo y de playa a la vez, que les hiciera desconectar del ritmo acelerado de la vida moderna. La arquitectura contemporánea de la construcción del arquitecto Damián Ribas fue el lienzo sobre el que Clara Joly d'Aussy se planteó dotar a la casa de calidez llevando el Mediterráneo y el verde del Empordá, hacia el interior. Para ello se valió de la madera en muebles y revestimientos, fibras naturales como el ratán, yute y esparto y los tonos beige y tierra. Uno de los mayores desafíos fue separar la cocina, el comedor y el salón. Para tamizar la luz y dividir estos espacios sin cerrarlos, la interiorista utilizó puertas correderas de lamas de madera, en vertical. Las mismas lamas, pero en horizontal, completan armarios y puertas interiores dándole a la casa una continuidad. La iluminación ha sido otro elemento estético clave: lámparas industriales mezcladas con ratán, y otras de papel, generan un ambiente cálido que combinado con la madera consiguen un espíritu de puro relax vacacional.

Photos: © Stella Rotger (Magazine «El Mueble») | Styling: Olga Gilbernet

D'AUSSY INTERIORS

Clara Joly d'Aussy

With a long international experience in the interior design sector, Clara Joly d'Aussy runs the studio she founded in 2017 with her father Dominique Joly d'Aussy, in Alt Empordà (Spain). The designer has collaborated with renowned architecture and interior design studios in Australia, such as Alexander and Co and the Japanese Koichi Takada, on residential and restoration projects. On her return to Barcelona, she settled in the Empordà, a region in Catalonia framed by the Mediterranean and the Pyrenees. Her second homes and new construction projects are focused on the Mediterranean style and the Catalan essence, integrating the environment and materials of the region.

Clara Joly d'Aussy verfügt über eine langjährige internationale Erfahrung im Bereich der Innenarchitektur und leitet das Studio, das sie 2017 zusammen mit ihrem Vater Dominique Joly d'Aussy in Alt Empordà (Spanien) gegründet hat. Der Designer hat mit renommierten Architektur- und Innenarchitekturbüros in Australien wie Alexander and Co und dem Japaner Koichi Takada an Wohn- und Restaurierungsprojekten zusammengearbeitet. Nach ihrer Rückkehr nach Barcelona ließ sie sich im Empordà nieder, einer Region in Katalonien, die vom Mittelmeer und den Pyrenäen eingerahmt wird. Seine Zweitwohnungen und Neubauprojekte sind auf den mediterranen Stil und das katalanische Wesen ausgerichtet und integrieren die Umgebung und die Materialien der Region.

Forte d'une longue expérience internationale dans le secteur de la décoration intérieure, Clara Joly d'Aussy dirige le studio qu'elle a fondé en 2017 avec son père Dominique Joly d'Aussy, dans l'Alt Empordà (Espagne). Le designer a collaboré avec des studios d'architecture et de décoration intérieure renommés en Australie, comme Alexander and Co et le Japonais Koichi Takada, sur des projets résidentiels et de restauration. De retour à Barcelone, elle s'installe dans l'Empordà, une région de Catalogne encadrée par la Méditerranée et les Pyrénées. Ses résidences secondaires et ses projets de construction neuve sont axés sur le style méditerranéen et l'essence catalane, en intégrant l'environnement et les matériaux de la région.

Con una larga experiencia internacional en el sector del interiorismo, Clara Joly d'Aussy dirige el estudio que fundó en el año 2017 con su padre Dominique Joly d'Aussy, en el Alt Empordà (España). La diseñadora ha colaborado con reputados estudios de arquitectura y diseño de interiores en Australia, como Alexander and Co y el japonés Koichi Takada, en proyectos residenciales y de restauración. A su regreso a Barcelona, se instaló en el Empordà, una región en Cataluña enmarcada por el Mediterráneo y los Pirineos. Sus proyectos de segundas residencias y obra nueva están enfocados al estilo mediterráneo y a la esencia catalana, integrando el entorno y los materiales de la región.

Risør, Norway

I/O CABIN

This Norwegian summer cabin elegantly bridges modernity and tradition, balancing coastal vernacular with contemporary design to embrace nature's simplicity.

Three separate volumes are connected by a wooden deck floating above the sloped terrain of solid rock. Under a shared, cantilevered roof, the atrium shaped floor plan creates an "inside/outside" effect for its purpose as a summer house - using the outdoor spaces as much as the indoors.
The summer cabin is wrapped in locally sourced spruce siding, impregnated with an organic wood protection with gray color pigments. The interior walls are all out of white painted, horizontal wood siding that meets a warmer toned floor and ceiling of white oiled spruce - typical to traditional and older cabins on the coast of Norway. The wooden pillars lifting the cabin off the ground are connected with cross-laminated timber beams in the deck, continuing all the way up to the roof construction which copies the structural beams in the deck. A V-shaped wood column caries the weight of the cantilevered roof as a large glass corner opens the main living space to its surrounding natural elements.

Trois volumes séparés sont reliés par une plateforme en bois flottant sur le terrain incliné de roche solide. Sous un toit en porte-à-faux partagé, le plan d'étage en forme d'atrium crée un effet « intérieur/extérieur » pour une utilisation en tant que maison d'été, utilisant les espaces extérieurs autant que les intérieurs.
La cabane d'été est enveloppée de sapin d'origine locale, imprégné d'une protection organique pour le bois avec des pigments de couleur grise. Les murs intérieurs sont tous en lambris de bois peint en blanc, qui rencontre un sol et un plafond de teinte plus chaude en sapin blanc huilé, typique des cabanes traditionnelles et anciennes de la côte norvégienne. Les piliers en bois surélevant la cabine du sol sont reliés par des poutres en bois lamellé-collé sur la plateforme, se poursuivant jusqu'à la structure du toit qui reproduit les poutres structurales sur la plateforme. Une colonne de bois en forme de V supporte le poids du toit en porte-à-faux tandis qu'une grande baie vitrée ouvre l'espace de vie principal à ses éléments naturels environnants.

Drei separate Volumina sind durch eine Plattform aus Holz verbunden, die über dem geneigten Gelände aus festem Fels schwebt. Unter einem gemeinsamen überhängenden Dach erzeugt der atriumförmige Grundriss einen „drinnen/draußen"-Effekt für die Nutzung als Sommerhaus, wobei die äußeren Räume ebenso wie die inneren genutzt werden.
Die Sommerhütte ist in einheimische Fichte gehüllt, die mit einem organischen Holzschutzmittel mit grauen Farbpigmenten imprägniert ist. Die Innenwände sind alle aus weiß gestrichener Holzverkleidung gefertigt, die auf einen wärmeren Ton von geölter weißer Fichte trifft, typisch für traditionelle und alte Hütten an der norwegischen Küste. Die Holzpfosten, die die Hütte vom Boden abheben, sind mit Brettschichtholzbalken auf der Plattform verbunden, die sich bis zur Dachstruktur fortsetzen, die die strukturellen Balken auf der Plattform kopiert. Eine V-förmige Holzsäule trägt das Gewicht des überhängenden Daches, während ein großes Fenster den Hauptwohnbereich zu seinen umgebenden natürlichen Elementen öffnet.

Tres volúmenes separados quedan conectados por una plataforma de madera que flota sobre el terreno inclinado de roca sólida. Bajo un techo compartido en voladizo, el plano de planta en forma de atrio crea un efecto «dentro/fuera» para su uso como casa de verano.
La cabaña de verano está envuelta de abeto de origen local, impregnado con una protección orgánica para madera con pigmentos de color gris. Las paredes interiores están todas hechas de revestimiento de madera pintada de blanco, que se encuentra con un suelo y techo de tono más cálido de abeto blanco aceitado, típico de cabañas tradicionales de la costa Noruega. Los pilares de madera que elevan la cabaña del suelo están conectados con vigas de madera contralaminada en la plataforma, continuando hasta la estructura del techo que copia las vigas estructurales en la plataforma. Una columna de madera en forma de V soporta el peso del techo en voladizo mientras que un gran ventanal abre el espacio de estar principal a sus elementos naturales circundantes.

Photos: © Carlos Rollán

ERLING BERG

Erling Berg

Norwegian born, Erling Berg is an architect and designer with a passion for crafting unique spaces addressing the important relationship between scale, form, light and the use of genuine materials, carefully considering context and functionality. With a rigorous and concept-driven approach, Berg focuses on timeless aesthetics, delicate details and simplicity within the built environment. Berg, who spent the majority of his twenties and his early thirties in California finds inspiration in the horizontal language of mid-century architecture from the region, as well as the Norwegian vernacular and its long building traditions, focusing on wood as the main structural, exterior and interior component.

Geboren in Norwegen, ist Erling Berg ein Architekt und Designer mit einer Leidenschaft für die Schaffung einzigartiger Räume, die die wichtige Beziehung zwischen Maßstab, Form, Licht und der Verwendung von authentischen Materialien ansprechen, wobei der Kontext und die Funktionalität sorgfältig berücksichtigt werden. Mit einem rigorosen und konzeptbasierten Ansatz konzentriert sich Berg auf zeitlose Ästhetik, feine Details und Einfachheit in der gebauten Umgebung. Berg, der den Großteil seiner Zwanziger und frühen Dreißigerjahre in Kalifornien verbracht hat, findet Inspiration in der horizontalen Sprache der Architektur der Mitte des 20. Jahrhunderts in der Region sowie im norwegischen Volksmund und seinen langen Bautraditionen, wobei Holz als Hauptstrukturkomponente sowohl im Außen- als auch im Innenbereich im Mittelpunkt steht.

Né en Norvège, Erling Berg est un architecte et designer passionné par la création d'espaces uniques qui explorent la relation importante entre l'échelle, la forme, la lumière et l'utilisation de matériaux authentiques, en tenant compte attentivement du contexte et de la fonctionnalité. Avec une approche rigoureuse et conceptuelle, Berg se concentre sur des esthétiques intemporelles, des détails délicats et la simplicité dans l'environnement bâti. Ayant passé la majeure partie de ses vingtaine et du début de ses trente ans en Californie, Berg trouve son inspiration dans le langage horizontal de l'architecture du milieu du XXe siècle de la région, ainsi que dans le vernaculaire norvégien et ses longues traditions de construction, mettant l'accent sur le bois comme composant structurel principal, tant à l'extérieur qu'à l'intérieur.

Nacido en Noruega, Erling Berg es un arquitecto y diseñador con una pasión por crear espacios únicos que aborden la importante relación entre la escala, la forma, la luz y el uso de materiales genuinos, considerando cuidadosamente el contexto y la funcionalidad. Con un enfoque riguroso y basado en conceptos, Berg se centra en estéticas atemporales, detalles delicados y simplicidad dentro del entorno construido. Berg, quien pasó la mayor parte de sus veinte años y principios de sus treinta en California, encuentra inspiración en el lenguaje horizontal de la arquitectura de mediados del siglo XX de la región, así como en el vernáculo noruego y sus largas tradiciones de construcción, centrándose en la madera como componente estructural principal, tanto exterior como interior.

Erling Berg's approach combines structural elegance with timeless design, weaving natural materials and thoughtful construction into a harmonious summer retreat.

CASA JUNGLA

A harmonious blend of local materials and thoughtful design, this home opens to the Costa Rican jungle, creating a seamless indoor-outdoor connection.

The design and conceptualization of Casa Jungla involve a continuous dialogue between the natural environment and the dwelling. Residents experience a transition between indoor and outdoor spaces by crossing thresholds that expose or shelter them in relation to nature. The house is distributed around a perimeter wall of local fieldstone, providing privacy while keeping the rear facade open to the landscape. The social program is concentrated on the ground floor, with a kitchen, living room, and dining room in a single space that opens up to views of the trees, the pool, and the terrace. The secondary bedrooms share a bathroom and are oriented towards outdoor spaces. On the lower level, a living area with access to the garden, laundry room, and equipment room is created. An additional level with concrete beams and an external staircase was incorporated, where the master bedroom with a bathroom, balcony, and planter is located. Openings at both ends provide natural light, cross ventilation, and views of the jungle.

La conception et la conceptualisation de la Casa Jungla découlent d'un dialogue continu entre l'environnement naturel et l'habitat. Les résidents vivent une transition entre les espaces intérieurs et extérieurs en traversant des seuils qui exposent ou protègent la relation avec la nature. La maison est distribuée autour d'un mur périmétral en pierre de mollejón local, assurant l'intimité tout en maintenant la façade arrière ouverte sur le paysage. Le programme se concentre au rez-de-chaussée, avec une cuisine, un salon et une salle à manger dans un espace ouvert offrant une vue sur les arbres, la piscine et la terrasse. Les chambres secondaires partagent une salle de bains et sont orientées vers les espaces extérieurs. Au niveau inférieur, une zone de séjour avec accès au jardin, une buanderie et une salle d'équipements sont créées. Un niveau supplémentaire avec des poutres en béton et un escalier extérieur est ajouté, abritant la chambre principale avec salle de bains, balcon et pot de fleurs. Des ouvertures aux deux extrémités fournissent une lumière naturelle, une ventilation croisée et des vues sur la jungle.

Das Design und die Konzeptualisierung des Casa Jungla basieren auf einem Dialog zwischen der natürlichen Umgebung und dem Wohnraum. Das Haus ist um eine Perimeterwand aus örtlichem Stein gebaut, die Privatsphäre bietet und die Rückseite des Hauses zum Landschaftspanorama hin offen lässt. Das Programm konzentriert sich im Erdgeschoss mit Küche, Wohnzimmer und Esszimmer in einem offenen Raum, der sich zur Aussicht auf Bäume, Pool und Terrasse hin öffnet. Die sekundären Schlafzimmer teilen sich ein Badezimmer und sind zum Außenbereich ausgerichtet. Auf der unteren Ebene befindet sich ein Wohnbereich mit Zugang zum Garten, zur Wäscherei und zum Maschinenraum. Eine zusätzliche Ebene mit Betonträgern und einer Außentreppe wurde hinzugefügt, auf der sich das Hauptschlafzimmer mit Bad, Balkon und Pflanzgefäß befindet. Öffnungen an beiden Enden bieten natürliches Licht, Querlüftung und Ausblicke auf den Dschungel.

El diseño y conceptualización de Casa Jungla parte un diálogo continuo entre el entorno natural y la vivienda. Los residentes experimentan una transición entre espacios interiores y exteriores al atravesar umbrales que exponen o resguardan la relación con la naturaleza. La casa se distribuye alrededor de un muro perimetral de piedra de mollejón local, proporcionando privacidad y manteniendo la fachada trasera abierta al paisaje. El programa se concentra en la planta baja, con cocina, sala y comedor en un espacio único que se abre hacia la vista de los árboles, la piscina y la terraza. Los dormitorios secundarios comparten un baño y se orientan hacia los espacios exteriores. En el nivel inferior se crea un área de estar con acceso al jardín, lavandería y sala de equipos. Se incorporó un nivel adicional con vigas de hormigón y escalera exterior, donde se encuentra el dormitorio principal con baño, balcón y maceta. Aperturas en ambos extremos proporcionan luz natural, ventilación cruzada y vistas a la jungla.

Photos: © Andrés García Lachner

FAMM ARQUITECTURA

Felipe Apestegui, Mariano Mesalles

FAMM Architecture, based in Costa Rica, specializes in residential, commercial, and hospitality projects in tropical environments, standing out for its excellence in design, sustainability, and work ethics. From initial sketches to final inspection, the FAMM team actively engages in all stages of the project, ensuring smooth execution and client satisfaction. Their focus on high-quality design is combined with sustainable practices, including passive techniques for energy efficiency and the use of local materials. Transparency and honesty are fundamental in their relationship with clients, working closely to tailor every aspect of the project to their needs and desires, aiming to exceed their expectations in terms of time, cost, and quality.

FAMM Architecture mit Sitz in Costa Rica ist auf Wohn-, Gewerbe- und Gastgewerbeprojekte in tropischen Umgebungen spezialisiert und zeichnet sich durch Exzellenz im Design, Nachhaltigkeit und ethisches Arbeiten aus. Vom ersten Entwurf bis zur endgültigen Inspektion ist das FAMM-Team in allen Projektphasen aktiv involviert und gewährleistet einen reibungslosen Ablauf und die Zufriedenheit der Kunden. Ihr Schwerpunkt auf hochwertigem Design wird mit nachhaltigen Praktiken kombiniert, einschließlich passiver Techniken zur Energieeffizienz und Verwendung lokaler Materialien. Transparenz und Ehrlichkeit sind grundlegend für ihre Beziehung zu den Kunden, indem sie eng zusammenarbeiten, um jeden Aspekt des Projekts an deren Bedürfnisse und Wünsche anzupassen und deren Erwartungen in Bezug auf Zeit, Kosten und Qualität zu übertreffen.

FAMM Architecture, basée au Costa Rica, est spécialisée dans les projets résidentiels, commerciaux et hôteliers dans les environnements tropicaux, se distinguant par son excellence en design, durabilité et éthique de travail. Des croquis initiaux à l'inspection finale, l'équipe de FAMM est activement impliquée à toutes les étapes du projet, garantissant une exécution fluide et la satisfaction du client. Leur approche de haute qualité en matière de conception est associée à des pratiques durables, y compris des techniques passives pour l'efficacité énergétique et l'utilisation de matériaux locaux. La transparence et l'honnêteté sont essentielles dans leur relation avec les clients, et ils s'efforcent d'établir des partenariats à long terme basés sur la confiance et le respect mutuel.

FAMM Architecture, con sede en Costa Rica, se especializa en proyectos residenciales, comerciales y de hospitalidad en entornos tropicales, destacándose por su excelencia en diseño, sostenibilidad y ética laboral. Desde los bocetos iniciales hasta la inspección final, el equipo de FAMM se involucra activamente en todas las etapas del proyecto, garantizando una ejecución fluida y la satisfacción del cliente. Su enfoque en diseño de alta calidad se combina con prácticas sostenibles, incluyendo técnicas pasivas para la eficiencia energética y el uso de materiales locales. La transparencia y la honestidad son fundamentales en su relación con los clientes, trabajando en estrecha colaboración para adaptar cada aspecto del proyecto a sus necesidades y deseos, con el objetivo de superar sus expectativas en tiempo, costo y calidad.

Natural materials and integrated landscaping highlight FAMM Architecture's commitment to sustainable design and a deep respect for the tropical environment.

LAKE SHORE PLACE

Neutral tones, natural materials, and eclectic textures shape a serene yet inviting home that redefines the slow life in Palm Beach.

The owners bought this house during the Covid pandemic, when they decided to replace the frenetic pace of New York City with the slow life of Palm Beach. Given the area's hot climate, the house had to be light and breezy, but also cosy. "They didn't want their house to look cold or austere, or like a holiday spot in Florida," explains Brittany Hakimfar, "that's why they were attracted to my interiors," adds the Far Sudio designer. Consequently, the aim was to create a space that was both timeless and eclectic. To achieve this, she resorted to neutral tones and the play of different textures with tone-on-tone. Broken whites, bone, and variations of sand, combined with pastels in the children's rooms, created a visual unity throughout much of the house. Natural stone and white oak finishes were also used. The exception was the study with anthracite grey walls that call for introspection. The studio designed all the bespoke joinery to make the most of the space and created large display windows to showcase ceramics and artwork.

Les propriétaires ont acheté cette maison pendant la pandémie de Covid, lorsqu'ils ont décidé de remplacer le rythme frénétique de New York par la vie lente de Palm Beach. Compte tenu du climat chaud de la région, la maison devait être légère et fraîche, mais aussi confortable. « Ils ne voulaient pas que leur maison ait l'air froide ou austère, ou qu'elle ressemble à un lieu de vacances en Floride », explique Brittany Hakimfar, « c'est pourquoi ils ont été attirés par mes intérieurs », ajoute la designer de Far Sudio. L'objectif était donc de créer un espace à la fois intemporel et éclectique. Pour y parvenir, elle a recouru à des tons neutres et au jeu des différentes textures en ton sur ton. Des blancs cassés, des os et des variations de sable, associés à des pastels dans les chambres d'enfants, ont créé une unité visuelle dans une grande partie de la maison. Des finitions en pierre naturelle et en chêne blanc ont également été utilisées. L'exception était le bureau aux murs gris anthracite qui appellent à l'introspection. Le studio a conçu toute la menuiserie sur mesure pour tirer le meilleur parti de l'espace et a créé de grandes fenêtres pour exposer les céramiques et les œuvres d'art.

Die Eigentümer kauften dieses Haus während der Covid-Pandemie, als sie beschlossen, das hektische Tempo von New York City durch das langsame Leben in Palm Beach zu ersetzen. In Anbetracht des heißen Klimas in der Region musste das Haus leicht und luftig, aber auch gemütlich sein. „Sie wollten nicht, dass ihr Haus kalt oder streng aussieht oder wie ein Urlaubsort in Florida," erklärt Brittany Hakimfar, „deshalb fühlten sie sich zu meiner Inneneinrichtung hingezogen," fügt die Far Sudio-Designerin hinzu. Das Ziel war also, einen Raum zu schaffen, der sowohl zeitlos als auch eklektisch ist. Um dies zu erreichen, griff sie auf neutrale Töne und das Spiel verschiedener Texturen mit Ton-in-Ton zurück. Gebrochenes Weiß, Knochen und Variationen von Sand, kombiniert mit Pastellfarben in den Kinderzimmern, schufen eine visuelle Einheit im gesamten Haus. Auch Naturstein und Weißeiche kamen zum Einsatz. Die Ausnahme war das Arbeitszimmer mit anthrazitgrauen Wänden, die zur Selbstbeobachtung einladen. Das Studio entwarf alle maßgefertigten Tischlerarbeiten, um den Raum optimal zu nutzen, und gestaltete große Schaufenster zur Präsentation von Keramik und Kunstwerken.

Los propietarios compraron esta casa durante la pandemia del Covid, cuando decidieron sustituir el ritmo frenético de la ciudad de Nueva York por el slow life de Palm Beach. En atención al clima caluroso de la zona, la casa debía tener un carácter ligero y fresco, pero también acogedor. «No querían que se su casa se viera fría o austera, o como un sitio para las vacaciones en Florida —explica Brittany Hakimfar— por eso se sintieron atraídos por mis interiores», añade la diseñadora de Far Sudio. El objetivo fue crear un espacio atemporal y ecléctico a la vez. Para ello recurrió a los tonos neutros y al juego de diferentes texturas con tono sobre tono. Blancos rotos, hueso, y variaciones de arena, combinados con pasteles en las habitaciones infantiles, generaron una unidad visual en gran parte de la vivienda. También utilizó acabados en piedra natural y roble blanco. La excepción fue el estudio con paredes en gris antracita que llaman a la introspección. El estudió diseñó toda la carpintería a medida con lo que aprovechó al máximo los espacios para generar amplios escaparates y exhibir piezas de cerámica y obras de arte de los propietarios.

Photos: © Brian Wetzel | Stylist: Kristi Hunter

FAR STUDIO

Brittany Hakimfar, Benjamin Hakimfar

Far Studio is dedicated to interior design in an organic modernist vein. Based in Philadelphia, but available internationally, the firm creates spaces where comfort and beauty reign. They describe their style as "West Coast design with an East Coast sensibility and a European twist." Brittany Hakimfar is the founder. After graduating from George Washington University with a degree in interior design, she began her career in New York working for Mark Cunningham. In 2012 she moved to Los Angeles to collaborate with renowned designer Waldo Fernandez, where she honed her skills in high-end residential and commercial design. She returned to Philadelphia to start her own design firm with her husband, Benjamin Hakimfar.

Far Studio widmet sich der Innenarchitektur im Stil der organischen Moderne. Das Unternehmen mit Sitz in Philadelphia, das aber auch international tätig ist, schafft Räume, in denen Komfort und Schönheit herrschen. Sie beschreiben ihren Stil als „Westküsten-Design mit einer Ostküsten-Sensibilität und einem europäischen Touch." Brittany Hakimfar ist die Gründerin. Nach ihrem Abschluss in Innenarchitektur an der George Washington University begann sie ihre Karriere in New York, wo sie für Mark Cunningham arbeitete. Im Jahr 2012 zog sie nach Los Angeles, um mit dem renommierten Designer Waldo Fernandez zusammenzuarbeiten, wo sie ihre Fähigkeiten im Bereich hochwertiges Wohn- und Geschäftsdesign verfeinerte. Sie kehrte nach Philadelphia zurück und gründete zusammen mit ihrem Mann Benjamin Hakimfar ihr eigenes Designbüro.

Far Studio se consacre à la décoration intérieure dans une veine moderniste et organique. Basé à Philadelphie, mais disponible à l'international, le cabinet crée des espaces où règnent confort et beauté. Ils décrivent leur style comme « un design de la côte ouest avec une sensibilité de la côte est et une touche européenne ». Brittany Hakimfar est la fondatrice. Après avoir obtenu un diplôme d'architecte d'intérieur à l'université George Washington, elle a commencé sa carrière à New York en travaillant pour Mark Cunningham. En 2012, elle s'est installée à Los Angeles pour collaborer avec le célèbre designer Waldo Fernandez, où elle a affiné ses compétences en matière de design résidentiel et commercial haut de gamme. Elle est retournée à Philadelphie pour créer sa propre agence de design avec son mari, Benjamin Hakimfar.

Far Studio se dedica al diseño de interiores en una vertiente modernista orgánica. Con sede en Filadelfia, pero disponible a nivel internacional, la firma crea espacios en los que impera la comodidad y la belleza. Describen a su estilo como «diseño de la Costa Oeste con una sensibilidad de la Costa Este y un toque europeo». Brittany Hakimfar es la fundadora. Después de graduarse en la Universidad George Washington en diseño de interiores, comenzó su carrera en Nueva York trabajando para Mark Cunningham. En 2012 se trasladó a Los Ángeles para colaborar con el reconocido diseñador Waldo Fernández, donde perfeccionó sus habilidades en el diseño residencial y comercial de alta gama. Regresó a Filadelfia para comenzar su propia empresa de diseño con su marido, Benjamin Hakimfar.

TOM FORD

VOGUE LIVING HOUSES GARDENS PEOPLE
at 100

Custom joinery and natural stone finishes highlight Far Studio's organic modernist approach, merging timeless elegance with comfortable living.

11701

RESIDENCE IN THE GALILEE

A tranquil retreat overlooking the Sea of Galilee, where sustainable design and thoughtful architecture harmonize with the natural landscape.

The house overlooks the Sea of Galilee with a sweeping view from every room. The generous openings, facing the view to the south and east, required shading and filtering against the intense sun provided by the wooden shutters. The shutters can slide in adjustment to the position of the sun, and privacy requirements. Sustainability and environmental considerations played a key role in the design of the house. To improve climate control, the windows and doors were recessed behind the wooden shutters, creating intermediate spaces, kind of outdoor rooms, which allow for sitting in the fresh country air while preserving privacy and intimacy of indoors. The design helps keeping the house cool and pleasant even during the hottest days of summer. The house was designed to blend into its pastoral environment. The rugged terrain and the surrounding olive and carob groves, where horses graze, have led to the choice of the house finishes, matching colours and materials for the cement-textured plaster and wooden shutters on the exterior, and light brown stone for the interior flooring and wooden ceiling.

La maison donne sur la mer de Galilée depuis chaque pièce. Les ouvertures généreuses, orientées au sud et à l'est, nécessitaient une protection et une filtration contre le soleil intense grâce à des volets en bois qui peuvent coulisser pour s'adapter à la position du soleil et aux besoins d'intimité. La durabilité et les considérations environnementales ont joué un rôle clé dans la conception de la maison. Pour améliorer la régulation du climat, les fenêtres et les portes ont été encastrées derrière les volets en bois, créant ainsi des espaces intermédiaires, des sortes de chambres à ciel ouvert, qui permettent de s'asseoir à l'air frais de la campagne tout en préservant l'intimité et la vie privée de l'intérieur. Cette conception permet de garder la maison fraîche et agréable même pendant les journées d'été les plus chaudes. La maison a été conçue pour se fondre dans son environnement bucolique. Le terrain vallonné et les oliveraies et caroubiers environnants, où paissent les chevaux, ont conduit au choix des finitions de la maison, des couleurs et matériaux assortis pour le plâtre à texture ciment et les volets en bois à l'extérieur, et de la pierre brun clair pour le sol intérieur et le plafond en bois.

Das Haus bietet von jedem Zimmer aus einen Blick auf den See Genezareth. Die großzügigen, nach Süden und Osten ausgerichteten Öffnungen erforderten eine Beschattung und Filterung gegen die intensive Sonne durch hölzerne Fensterläden, die sich je nach Sonnenstand und Sichtschutzbedarf verschieben lassen. Nachhaltigkeit und Umweltaspekte spielten bei der Gestaltung des Hauses eine wichtige Rolle. Um die Klimatisierung zu verbessern, wurden Fenster und Türen hinter den hölzernen Fensterläden versenkt. So entstanden Zwischenräume, eine Art Freiluftzimmer, in denen man sich an der frischen Landluft aufhalten kann, ohne die Intimität und Privatsphäre des Innenraums zu verlieren. Die Konstruktion trägt dazu bei, dass das Haus auch an den heißesten Sommertagen kühl und angenehm bleibt. Das Haus wurde so entworfen, dass es sich in seine ländliche Umgebung einfügt. Das hügelige Gelände und die umliegenden Olivenhaine und Johannisbrotbäume, auf denen die Pferde weiden, haben zur Wahl der Oberflächen des Hauses geführt: passende Farben und Materialien für den Zementputz und die hölzernen Fensterläden an der Außenseite und hellbrauner Stein für den Innenboden und die Holzdecke.

La casa tiene vistas al mar de Galilea desde todas las habitaciones. Las generosas aberturas, orientadas al sur y al este, requerían sombra y filtración contra el intenso sol gracias a las contraventanas de madera que pueden deslizarse para adaptarse a la posición del sol y a las necesidades de privacidad. La sostenibilidad y las consideraciones medioambientales desempeñaron un papel clave en el diseño de la vivienda. Para mejorar el control climático, las ventanas y puertas se empotraron detrás de las contraventanas de madera, creando espacios intermedios, una especie de habitaciones al aire libre, que permiten sentarse al aire fresco del campo preservando la intimidad y privacidad del interior. El diseño ayuda a mantener la casa fresca y agradable incluso durante los días más calurosos del verano. La casa se diseñó para integrarse en su entorno bucólico. El terreno accidentado y los olivares y algarrobos circundantes, donde pastan los caballos, han propiciado la elección de los acabados de la casa, colores y materiales a juego para el enlucido con textura de cemento y las contraventanas de madera del exterior, y piedra marrón claro para el suelo interior y el techo de madera.

Photos: © Amit Geron, Golany Architects

GOLANY ARCHITECTS

Yaron Golany, Galit Golany

Golany Architects is an award-winning design practice based in Tel Aviv. Its principals are the husband and wife team, Yaron Golany and Galit Golany. Their projects are characterized by a strong response to the context, with its cultural and environmental aspects. This results in work that is varied in its formal and material qualities. The projects also vary in size and program, from a 45 m^2 residence to a 45,000 m^2 high-tech campus, and include office buildings, residencial buildings, public buildings, landscape and urban design.

Golany Architects ist ein preisgekröntes Designbüro in Tel Aviv, das von dem Ehepaar Yaron Golany und Galit Golany geleitet wird. Ihre Projekte zeichnen sich durch eine starke Reaktion auf den Kontext, seine kulturellen und ökologischen Aspekte aus. Das Ergebnis sind Arbeiten, die in ihren formalen und materiellen Qualitäten vielfältig sind. Die Projekte sind von unterschiedlicher Größe und Programmatik, von einem 45 m^2 großen Wohnhaus bis zu einem 45 000 m^2 großen High-Tech-Campus, und umfassen Büro-, Wohn-, öffentliche, Landschafts- und Stadtplanungsprojekte.

Golany Architects est un studio de design primé de Tel Aviv, dirigé par l'équipe mari et femme Yaron Golany et Galit Golany. Leurs projets se caractérisent par une forte réaction au contexte, à ses aspects culturels et environnementaux. Le résultat est un travail varié dans ses qualités formelles et matérielles. Les projets sont également variés en termes de taille et de programme, allant d'une résidence de 45 m^2 à un campus high-tech de 45 000 m^2, et comprennent des immeubles de bureaux, des projets résidentiels, publics, paysagers et d'aménagement urbain.

Golany Architects es un galardonado estudio de diseño de Tel Aviv, dirigido por el matrimonio formado por Yaron Golany y Galit Golany. Sus proyectos se caracterizan por una fuerte respuesta al contexto, sus aspectos culturales y medioambientales. El resultado es un trabajo variado en sus cualidades formales y materiales. Los proyectos también son diversos en tamaño y programa, desde una residencia de 45 m^2 a un campus de alta tecnología de 45.000 m^2, e incluyen edificios de oficinas, residenciales, públicos, proyectos paisajísticos y de diseño urbano.

Sliding wooden shutters and recessed openings define this residence, illustrating Golany Architects' commitment to environmental sensitivity and contextual harmony.

PENTHOUSE DAVOS

Natural materials, thoughtful layouts, and a touch of alpine elegance make this Swiss retreat a true home away from home.

"A home connected to a place and filled with the love of family and friends." With this in mind, we were able to design an exclusive vacation apartment, which impresses with its timeless alpine chic. A 6-room apartment has been created on an area of approx. 380 m², in which each room has its own en-suite bathroom. The residents and their guests were to be given the feeling of being in a home away from home. The area for social interaction was skillfully separated from the sleeping areas, creating a sense of increased privacy for vacation guests in particular. The area of the apartment where everyone comes together has been divided up very generously, with the kitchen and the transverse fireplace acting as a room divider and allowing more coziness. With carefully selected materials that create a connection to the beautiful natural surroundings of the Swiss mountains, rooms full of positive energy and relaxed power have been created.

« Un foyer connecté à un lieu et rempli de l'amour de la famille et des amis ». Avec cela à l'esprit, nous avons été en mesure de concevoir un appartement exclusif de vacances, qui impressionne par son style alpin intemporel chic. Un appartement de 6 pièces a été créé sur une superficie d'environ 380 m², où chaque chambre a sa propre salle de bain. Les résidents et leurs invités devaient se sentir comme chez eux loin de chez eux. La zone d'interaction sociale a été habilement séparée des zones de couchage, créant une sensation d'intimité accrue, surtout pour les vacanciers. La zone de l'appartement où tout le monde se réunit a été généreusement divisée, avec la cuisine et la cheminée transversale agissant comme séparateurs d'espaces et permettant une plus grande intimité. Avec des matériaux soigneusement sélectionnés qui créent un lien avec le magnifique environnement naturel des montagnes suisses, des chambres pleines d'énergie positive et de pouvoir relaxant ont été créées.

„Ein Zuhause, das mit einem Ort verbunden ist und voller Liebe von Familie und Freunden ist." Mit diesem Gedanken im Hinterkopf konnten wir ein exklusives Ferienapartment entwerfen, das durch seinen zeitlosen alpinen Chic besticht. Es wurde ein Apartment mit 6 Zimmern auf einer Fläche von ca. 380 m² geschaffen, in dem jedes Zimmer über ein eigenes Badezimmer verfügt. Die Bewohner und ihre Gäste sollten das Gefühl haben, sich in einem Zuhause fernab von zu Hause zu befinden. Der soziale Interaktionsbereich wurde geschickt von den Schlafbereichen getrennt, um ein größeres Gefühl von Privatsphäre zu schaffen, insbesondere für Urlaubsgäste. Der Bereich der Wohnung, in dem sich alle versammeln, wurde großzügig unterteilt, wobei die Küche und der quer liegende Kamin als Raumteiler fungieren und eine größere Intimität ermöglichen. Durch sorgfältig ausgewählte Materialien, die eine Verbindung zur wunderschönen natürlichen Umgebung der Schweizer Berge herstellen, wurden Räume voller positiver Energie und entspannender Kraft geschaffen.

«Un hogar conectado a un lugar y lleno del amor de la familia y los amigos». Con esto en mente, hemos sido capaces de diseñar un exclusivo apartamento de vacaciones, que impresiona por su estilo atemporal chic alpino. Se ha creado un apartamento de 6 habitaciones en una superficie aproximada de 380 m², en el que cada habitación tiene su propio cuarto de baño. Los residentes y sus invitados debían tener la sensación de estar en un hogar lejos de casa. El área de interacción social se separó hábilmente de las zonas de dormitorio, creando una sensación de mayor intimidad, sobre todo para los huéspedes de vacaciones. La zona del apartamento donde se reúne todo el mundo se ha dividido de forma muy generosa, con la cocina y la chimenea transversal actuando como separador de ambientes y permitiendo una mayor intimidad. Con materiales cuidadosamente seleccionados que crean una conexión con el bello entorno natural de las montañas suizas, se han conseguido habitaciones llenas de energía positiva y poder relajante.

Photos: © Pierre Kellenberger

GO INTERIORS

Nicole Gottschall

For us, personal happiness means making other people happier and more satisfied within their homes. It is a privilege for us to be able to live our vocation as a profession. With dedication and joy to beauty, we are able to tailor each and every one of our projects to the needs of the residents and implement them with love down to the last detail. The focus of our work is the holistic view of a space, always in connection with the people for whom it is intended. We ensure that sensuality, harmony and haptic experiences create unique moments of well-being. We compose light and space, materials, colours and shapes, details and transitions into an overall picture.

Für uns bedeutet persönliches Glück, andere Menschen glücklicher und zufriedener in ihren Häusern zu machen. Es ist für uns ein Privileg, unsere Berufung als Beruf ausüben zu können. Mit Hingabe und Freude an der Schönheit sind wir in der Lage, jeden unserer Projekte an die Bedürfnisse der Bewohner anzupassen und sie bis ins kleinste Detail mit Liebe umzusetzen. Im Mittelpunkt unserer Arbeit steht die ganzheitliche Vision eines Raumes, immer in Verbindung mit den Menschen, für die er bestimmt ist. Wir stellen sicher, dass Sinnlichkeit, Harmonie und taktile Erfahrungen einzigartige Wohlfühlmomente schaffen. Wir komponieren Licht und Raum, Materialien, Farben und Formen, Details und Übergänge zu einem Gesamtbild.

Pour nous, le bonheur personnel signifie rendre les autres plus heureux et plus satisfaits dans leurs foyers. Pour nous, c'est un privilège de pouvoir vivre notre vocation en tant que profession. Avec dévouement et joie pour la beauté, nous sommes capables d'adapter chacun de nos projets aux besoins des résidents et de les réaliser avec amour jusqu'au moindre détail. Le centre de notre travail est la vision globale d'un espace, toujours en connexion avec les personnes auxquelles il est destiné. Nous nous assurons que la sensualité, l'harmonie et les expériences tactiles créent des moments uniques de bien-être. Nous composons la lumière et l'espace, les matériaux, les couleurs et les formes, les détails et les transitions dans une image d'ensemble.

Para nosotros, la felicidad personal significa hacer que otras personas sean más felices y estén más satisfechas en sus hogares. Para nosotros es un privilegio poder vivir nuestra vocación como profesión. Con dedicación y alegría por la belleza, somos capaces de adaptar todos y cada uno de nuestros proyectos a las necesidades de los residentes y llevarlos a cabo con amor hasta el último detalle. El centro de nuestro trabajo es la visión global de un espacio, siempre en conexión con las personas a las que va destinado. Nos aseguramos de que la sensualidad, la armonía y las experiencias táctiles creen momentos únicos de bienestar. Componemos luz y espacio, materiales, colores y formas, detalles y transiciones en una imagen de conjunto.

The seamless integration of natural textures and generous social spaces highlights the studio's passion for creating harmonious, uplifting environments.

Vĩnh Phúc, Vietnam

AJISAI HILL HOUSE

Perched on a mountainside, this residence merges traditional Vietnamese elements with contemporary design, creating a harmonious retreat amid the Tam Dao range.

The house is situated on a steep mountain slope, overlooking a vast valley with a view of a golf course and the Tam Dao mountain range. The goal is seamless integration with the surrounding natural landscape. The space should accommodate an extended family with 5 bedrooms and additional auxiliary spaces.
The main house is constructed with a steel frame finished with stone and natural wood, sheltering the house from the impact of drastic weather conditions in the area. The use of wood and expansive awnings draws inspiration from traditional Vietnamese architectural spaces, featuring rows of columns and symmetrical spaces. The main traffic axis is centrally balanced between the house and the various open spaces, connecting the front yard to the rear. The spaces between the elevated levels gradually open up new vistas, linking with the project's backdrop.The garden and the roof of the garage block are connected, expanding the flower planting area.

Das Haus liegt an einem steilen Bergabhang und ist auf ein weites Tal mit Blick auf einen Golfplatz und die Tam Dao Gebirgskette ausgerichtet. Der Raum soll eine erweiterte Familie mit fünf Schlafzimmern und zusätzlichen Nebenräumen unterbringen.
Das Haupthaus ist mit einem Stahlrahmen fertiggestellt, der mit Naturstein und Holz versehen ist und das Haus vor den Auswirkungen der drastischen Wetterbedingungen in der Region schützt. Die Verwendung von Holz und ausladenden Vordächern ist von traditionellen vietnamesischen architektonischen Räumen inspiriert, mit Reihen von Säulen und symmetrischen Räumen. Die Hauptverkehrsachse ist zentral zwischen dem Haus und den verschiedenen offenen Räumen ausbalanciert und verbindet die Vorder- mit der Rückseite des Hauses. Die Zwischenräume zwischen den Ebenen öffnen sich allmählich zu neuen Ausblicken und verbinden sich mit dem Hintergrund des Projekts. Der Garten und das Dach des Garagenblocks sind miteinander verbunden und erweitern die Blumenpflanzzone.

Ajisai Hill est située sur une pente de montagne abrupte, orientée vers une vaste vallée avec vue sur un terrain de golf et la chaîne de montagnes de Tam Dao. L'objectif est de s'intégrer parfaitement dans le paysage naturel environnant. L'espace doit accueillir une famille élargie avec cinq chambres et des espaces auxiliaires supplémentaires.
La maison principale est construite avec un cadre en acier fini avec de la pierre et du bois naturel, protégeant la maison de l'impact des conditions climatiques drastiques de la région. L'utilisation de bois et de auvents expansifs s'inspire des espaces architecturaux traditionnels vietnamiens, avec des rangées de colonnes et des espaces symétriques. L'axe de circulation principal est équilibré au centre entre la maison et les divers espaces ouverts, reliant le patio avant à l'arrière. Les espaces entre les niveaux s'ouvrent progressivement sur de nouvelles vues, se liant au fond du projet. Le jardin et le toit du bloc de garage sont connectés, élargissant la zone de plantation de fleurs.

La casa está situada en una pendiente de montaña empinada, orientada a un amplio valle con vistas a un campo de golf y la cordillera de Tam Dao. El objetivo es integrarse perfectamente con el paisaje natural circundante. El espacio debe dar cabida a una familia extendida con cinco dormitorios y espacios auxiliares adicionales.
La casa principal está construida con un marco de acero acabado con piedra y madera natural, protegiendo la casa del impacto de las condiciones climáticas drásticas en la zona. El uso de madera y toldos expansivos se inspira en los espacios arquitectónicos tradicionales vietnamitas, con filas de columnas y espacios simétricos. El eje de tráfico principal está equilibrado centralmente entre la casa y los diversos espacios abiertos, conectando el patio delantero con el trasero. Los espacios entre los niveles elevados gradualmente abren nuevas vistas, vinculándose con el fondo del proyecto. El jardín y el techo del bloque de garaje están conectados, ampliando la zona de plantación de flores.

Photos: © Triệu Chiên

IDEE ARCHITECTS

Trần Ngọc Linh, Nguyen Huy Hai

Founded in 2010, IDEE Architects was established by architects Tran Ngoc Linh and Nguyen Huy Hai, known for their design projects in resorts and residential homes. Over the years, the office has gained recognition with numerous awards and many projects featured in specialized magazines worldwide.
Our design philosophy, "Simplicity," focuses on purity and simplicity in architecture. IDEE practices architecture on projects ranging from small to large scales. We are committed to sustainability, nature, and considerate of the impact of design on environmental improvement and human awareness. We also prioritize the application of advanced solutions and new materials to explore the future direction of architecture.

Gegründet im Jahr 2010, wurde IDEE Architects von den Architekten Tran Ngoc Linh und Nguyen Huy Hai etabliert, die für ihre Designprojekte in Resorts und Wohnhäusern bekannt sind. Im Laufe der Jahre hat das Büro mit zahlreichen Preisen Anerkennung gefunden und viele Projekte wurden in Fachzeitschriften auf der ganzen Welt vorgestellt.
Unsere Designphilosophie, „Einfachheit," konzentriert sich auf die Reinheit und Einfachheit in der Architektur. IDEE praktiziert Architektur in Projekten von klein bis groß. Wir sind verpflichtet, Nachhaltigkeit, Natur und den Einfluss des Designs auf die Umweltverbesserung und das menschliche Bewusstsein zu berücksichtigen. Wir priorisieren auch die Anwendung fortschrittlicher Lösungen und neuer Materialien, um die zukünftige Richtung der Architektur zu erkunden.

IDEE Architects, fondé en 2010 par les architectes Tran Ngoc Linh et Nguyen Huy Hai, est connu pour ses projets de design dans les stations balnéaires et les maisons résidentielles. Au fil des ans, le cabinet a remporté de nombreux prix et a vu de nombreux projets présentés dans des magazines spécialisés du monde entier.
Notre philosophie de design, « Simplicité », se concentre sur la pureté et la simplicité en architecture. IDEE pratique l'architecture dans des projets allant de petite à grande échelle. Nous sommes engagés envers la durabilité, la nature et nous considérons l'impact de la conception sur l'amélioration de l'environnement et la conscience humaine. Nous donnons également la priorité à l'application de solutions avancées et de nouveaux matériaux pour explorer la direction future de l'architecture.

Fundada en 2010, IDEE Architects fue establecida por los arquitectos Tran Ngoc Linh y Nguyen Huy Hai, conocidos por sus proyectos de diseño en resorts y casas residenciales. A lo largo de los años, la oficina ha ganado reconocimiento con numerosos premios y muchos proyectos presentados en revistas especializadas en todo el mundo.
Nuestra filosofía de diseño, «Simplicidad», se centra en la pureza y simplicidad en la arquitectura. IDEE practica la arquitectura en proyectos que van desde pequeña a gran escala. Estamos comprometidos con la sostenibilidad, la naturaleza y consideramos el impacto del diseño en la mejora ambiental y la conciencia humana. También priorizamos la aplicación de soluciones avanzadas y nuevos materiales para explorar la dirección futura de la arquitectura.

Wooden columns, expansive awnings, and strategic garden connections reflect IDEE Architects' commitment to integrating natural beauty with architectural simplicity.

THELIFE SHIBUYA

Discover a harmonious blend of light, space, and craftsmanship where I IN's innovative design redefines luxury living in a Tokyo apartment.

I IN was commissioned to give a new life to this 40-year-old flat, under the THELIFE concept of the Good Life real estate group. With an aesthetic that calls for calm and essentials, the Japanese firm proposes a new way of living with a sense of sophistication and luxury. As soon as you walk through the front door, an abstract volume of natural light welcomes you and reveals space after space, different layers of experiences. In the foyer, a floral piece unfolds above the door, and a solid wood bench taken from a single cherry tree, stands in the warm light. The predominant tone is pale oak combined with lead grey fittings for a light aesthetic. Wavy glass panels replicate daylight from the bathroom to the entrance. White walls and ceilings highlight the edges of the softly rounded furniture in a nod to the wooden pillars of Japanese temple architecture. The rooms are connected from a minimalist open plan layout. The lines are clean with handle-free doors and furniture, and lighting is concealed in the walls or above the windows.

I IN a été chargé d'insuffler une nouvelle vie à cet appartement vieux de 40 ans dans le cadre du concept THELIFE du groupe immobilier Good Life. Avec une esthétique qui appelle au calme et à l'essentiel, la firme japonaise propose une nouvelle façon de vivre avec un sens de la sophistication et du luxe. Dès que vous franchissez la porte d'entrée, un volume abstrait de lumière naturelle vous accueille et vous révèle espace après espace, différentes couches d'expériences. Dans le foyer, une pièce florale se déploie au-dessus de la porte, et un banc en bois massif provenant d'un seul cerisier se dresse dans la lumière chaude. Le ton prédominant est le chêne clair combiné à des accessoires gris plomb pour une esthétique légère. Des panneaux de verre ondulés reproduisent la lumière du jour de la salle de bains à l'entrée. Les murs et les plafonds blancs soulignent les bords des meubles doucement arrondis, en clin d'œil aux piliers en bois de l'architecture des temples japonais. Les chambres sont reliées entre elles par un plan ouvert minimaliste. Les lignes sont épurées, avec des portes et des meubles sans poignée, et l'éclairage est dissimulé dans les murs ou au-dessus des fenêtres.

I IN wurde beauftragt, dieser 40 Jahre alten Wohnung im Rahmen des THELIFE-Konzepts der Immobiliengruppe Good Life neues Leben einzuhauchen. Mit einer Ästhetik, die nach Ruhe und Wesentlichkeit ruft, schlägt das japanische Unternehmen eine neue Art des Wohnens mit einem Gefühl von Raffinesse und Luxus vor. Sobald man durch die Eingangstür tritt, empfängt einen ein abstraktes Volumen aus natürlichem Licht und offenbart einen Raum nach dem anderen, verschiedene Schichten von Erfahrungen. Im Foyer entfaltet sich ein Blumenschmuck über der Tür, und eine Massivholzbank, die von einem einzelnen Kirschbaum stammt, steht im warmen Licht. Der vorherrschende Farbton ist helle Eiche in Kombination mit bleigrauen Beschlägen für eine leichte Ästhetik. Gewellte Glaspaneele lassen das Tageslicht vom Bad in die Küche fallen. Weiße Wände und Decken betonen die Kanten der sanft gerundeten Möbel in Anlehnung an die Holzsäulen der japanischen Tempelarchitektur. Die Zimmer sind durch einen minimalistischen, offenen Grundriss miteinander verbunden. Die Linienführung ist klar, Türen und Möbel sind grifflos, und die Beleuchtung ist in den Wänden oder über den Fenstern versteckt.

I IN se encargó de dar una nueva vida a este piso de 40 años de antigüedad, bajo el concepto de THELIFE del grupo inmobiliario Good Life. Con una estética que llama a la calma y a lo esencial, la firma japonesa propone una nueva forma de vivir con una sensación de sofisticación y lujo. Apenas se atraviesa la puerta principal, un volumen abstracto de luz natural da la bienvenida y revela espacio tras espacio, diferentes capas de experiencias. En el vestíbulo, una pieza floral se despliega sobre la puerta, y un banco de madera maciza extraída de un solo cerezo, se alza bajo la cálida luz. El tono predominante es el roble pálido que se combina con accesorios de color gris plomo para lograr una estética ligera. Los paneles de vidrio ondulado replican la luz del día desde el cuarto de baño a la entrada. Las paredes y los techos de color blanco resaltan los bordes de los muebles suavemente redondeados en un guiño a los pilares de madera de la arquitectura de los templos japoneses. Las habitaciones se conectan a partir de un esquema minimalista de planta abierta. Las líneas son limpias con puertas y muebles sin tiradores, y la iluminación está oculta en las paredes o sobre las ventanas.

Photos: © Norihito Yamauchi

I IN

Yohei Terui, Hiromu Yuyama

I IN Inc. is a Tokyo-based design studio founded in 2018 by Yohei Terui and Hiromu Yuyama. The firm is focused on finding innovative solutions in the design of spaces, and proposes striking and surprising interiors. Yohei graduated in Interior Design from Parsons School of Design in New York, after attending Meiji University in Tokyo. Between 2009 and 2017, he worked at Curiosity as a senior designer and before that at New York-based Gabellini Sheppard and SHoP Architects. Hiromu studied architecture and interior design at ICS College of Arts, graduated from Tokyo Gakugei University and worked at Curiosity as a senior designer. Previously, he worked at ILYA in Tokyo.

I IN Inc. ist ein Designstudio mit Sitz in Tokio, das 2018 von Yohei Terui und Hiromu Yuyama gegründet wurde. Das Unternehmen konzentriert sich auf die Suche nach innovativen Lösungen für die Gestaltung von Räumen und schlägt auffallende und überraschende Innenräume vor. Yohei machte seinen Abschluss in Innenarchitektur an der Parsons School of Design in New York, nachdem er die Meiji University in Tokio besucht hatte. Zwischen 2009 und 2017 arbeitete er als Senior Designer bei Curiosity und davor bei Gabellini Sheppard und SHoP Architects in New York. Hiromu studierte Architektur und Innenarchitektur am ICS College of Arts, machte seinen Abschluss an der Tokyo Gakugei University und arbeitete bei Curiosity als Senior Designer. Zuvor arbeitete er bei ILYA in Tokio.

I IN Inc. est un studio de design basé à Tokyo, fondé en 2018 par Yohei Terui et Hiromu Yuyama. Le cabinet s'attache à trouver des solutions innovantes dans la conception des espaces, et propose des intérieurs saisissants et surprenants. Yohei est diplômé en design d'intérieur de la Parsons School of Design de New York, après avoir fréquenté l'université Meiji de Tokyo. Entre 2009 et 2017, il a travaillé chez Curiosity en tant que concepteur principal et, avant cela, chez Gabellini Sheppard et SHoP Architects, basés à New York. Hiromu a étudié l'architecture et la décoration d'intérieur à l'ICS College of Arts, a obtenu un diplôme de l'université Tokyo Gakugei et a travaillé chez Curiosity en tant que designer principal. Auparavant, il a travaillé chez ILYA à Tokyo.

I IN Inc. es un estudio de diseño con sede en Tokio fundado en 2018 por Yohei Terui y Hiromu Yuyama. La firma se orienta a la búsqueda de soluciones innovadoras en el diseño de espacios, y propone interiores impactantes y sorprendentes. Yohei se licenció en Diseño de Interiores en la Parsons School of Design de Nueva York, tras pasar por la Universidad Meiji de Tokio. Entre 2009 y 2017, trabajó en Curiosity como diseñador principal y antes trabajó en las empresas neoyorquinas Gabellini Sheppard y SHoP Architects. Hiromu por su parte, estudió arquitectura y diseño de interiores en el ICS College of Arts. También se graduó en la Universidad Gakugei de Tokio y trabajó en Curiosity como diseñador principal. Anteriormente, trabajó en ILYA en Tokio.

Natural tones and soft contours shape an inviting environment, reflecting I IN's mastery in merging minimalism with the warmth of Japanese tradition.

CASCADA HOUSE

Modern architecture meets Mediterranean charm, blending natural textures, sustainable design, and light-filled spaces into a harmonious retreat.

The house is a perfect conjunction of modern architectural lines and the organic imperfections of the Mediterranean. Lime patches, rounded edges, and high-tech lighting combine and enhance the beauty of nature from sunrise to sunset. Inside the house, the feeling is that of being surrounded by open spaces that embrace the warm Mediterranean atmosphere. Despite the high ceilings and the maximalism of the architecture, you never have the impression of being alone. Decorative pieces and furniture from different parts of the world add richness and remind you that traveling through the window is possible. Stone walls embrace and minimize the impact of the architecture to merge the mountain with the building. Natural light pours into the interior creating environments defined by warm materials and natural textures. The main pillars of the concept are sustainability and beauty. Their savoir-vivre has created a perfect bubble of aesthetics and comfort, with well-being and joy in mind.

La maison est une conjonction parfaite entre les lignes architecturales modernes et les imperfections organiques de la Méditerranée. Des taches de chaux, des bords arrondis et un éclairage de haute techno- logie se combinent pour mettre en valeur la beauté de la nature, du lever au coucher du soleil. À l'intérieur de la maison, le sentiment est celui d'être entouré d'espaces ouverts qui embrassent la chaude atmosphère méditerranéenne. Malgré les hauts plafonds et le maximalisme de l'architecture, vous n'avez jamais l'impression d'être seul. Les pièces décoratives et les meubles provenant de différentes parties du monde ajoutent de la richesse et vous rappellent qu'il est possible de voyager par la fenêtre. Les murs de pierre embrassent et minimisent l'impact de l'architecture afin de fusionner la montagne avec le bâtiment. La lumière naturelle se déverse dans l'intérieur, créant des environnements définis par des matériaux chaleureux et des textures naturelles. Les principaux piliers du concept de cette maison sont la durabilité et la beauté. Leur savoir-vivre a créé une bulle parfaite d'esthétique et de confort, dans un souci de bien-être et de joie.

Das Haus ist eine perfekte Verbindung von modernen architektonis- chen Linien und den organischen Unvollkommenheiten des Mittel— meers. Kalkflecken, abgerundete Kanten und Hightech-Beleuchtung sorgen dafür, dass die Schönheit der Natur von Sonnenaufgang bis Sonnenuntergang zur Geltung kommt. Im Inneren des Hauses hat man das Gefühl, von offenen Räumen umgeben zu sein, die die warme mediterrane Atmosphäre einfangen. Trotz der hohen Decken und des Maximalismus der Architektur hat man nie das Gefühl, allein zu sein. Dekorationsgegenstände und Möbel aus verschiedenen Teilen der Welt bereichern den Raum und erinnern daran, dass eine Reise durch das Fenster möglich ist. Steinmauern umschließen die Architektur und minimieren deren Auswirkungen, um den Berg mit dem Gebäude zu verschmelzen. Natürliches Licht fällt in die Innenräume und schafft Umgebungen, die von warmen Materialien und natürlichen Texturen geprägt sind. Die wichtigsten Säulen des Konzepts sind Nachhaltigkeit und Schönheit. Ihr Savoir-vivre hat eine perfekte Mischung aus Ästhetik und Komfort geschaffen, in der Wohlbefinden und Freude im Vordergrund stehen.

La casa es una conjunción perfecta de las líneas arquitectónicas modernas y las imperfecciones orgánicas del Mediterráneo. Las manchas de cal, los bordes redondeados y la iluminación de alta tecnología, se combinan y potencian la belleza de la naturaleza, desde el amanecer hasta el atardecer. Dentro de la casa, la sensación es la de estar rodeado de espacios abiertos que abrazan el cálido ambiente mediterráneo. A pesar de los altos techos y el maximalismo de la arquitectura, nunca se tiene la impresión de estar solo. Las piezas de decoración y los muebles provenientes de diferentes lugares del mundo aportan riqueza y recuerdan que viajar a través de la ventana es posible. Los muros de piedra abrazan y minimizan el impacto de la arquitectura para fusionar la montaña con la construcción. La luz natural se cuela en el interior creando ambientes definidos por materiales cálidos y texturas naturales. Los principales pilares del concepto se esta vivienda son la sos- tenibilidad y la belleza. Su *savoir-vivre* ha creado una burbuja perfecta de estética y confort, pensando en el bienestar y la alegría.

Photos: © Gonzalo Moreno | Web: villacascada.es | Architect: Borja Donderis Pastor | Builder: Team Tip-Top

JESSICA BATAILLE - THE LIFESTYLE COMPANY

Jessica Bataille

The Jessica Bataille firm was born from the shop – Rust&Co – that the designer established in 1996, when she was 20. At that time, she was a pioneer in transforming Mexican-style furniture with great success. After 25 years, the company has nine companies and more than 60 professionals in architecture, art, design, and engineering. At Jessica Bataille, respect for the environment and sustainability are hallmarks, translated into the Passivhaus. This greenhouse standard aims to create highly energy-efficient homes using advanced insulation and air-sealing techniques. The firm is a Mediterranean reference in architecture and design and promotes the Jávea lifestyle, local craftsmanship, and culture.

Das Unternehmen Jessica Bataille ist aus dem Geschäft Rust&Co- hervorgegangen, das die Designerin 1996 im Alter von 20 Jahren gründete. Zu dieser Zeit war sie eine Pionierin im Transformieren von Möbeln im me- xikanischen Stil, und das mit großem Erfolg. Nach 25 Jahren zählt das Unternehmen neun Unternehmen und mehr als 60 Fachleute in den Bereichen Architektur, Kunst, Design und Technik. Bei Jessica Bataille sind Respekt vor der Umwelt und Nachhaltigkeit Markenzeichen, die sich im Passivhaus widerspiegeln, ein Green-Building-Standard, der darauf abzielt, hochgradig energieeffiziente Gebäude mit fortschrittlichen Isolierungs- und Luftabdichtungstechniken zu schaffen. Das Unternehmen ist eine mediterrane Referenz nicht nur für Architektur und Design, sondern auch für die Förderung des Lebensstils von Jávea, der lokalen Handwerkskunst und Kultur.

Le Studio Jessica Bataille est née de la boutique – Rust&Co – que la créatrice a créée en 1996, alors qu'elle avait 20 ans. À cette époque, elle était une pionnière dans la transformation de meubles de style mexicain, avec un grand succès. Après 25 ans, l'entreprise compte neuf sociétés et plus de 60 professionnels en architecture, art, design et ingénierie. Chez Jessica Bataille, le respect de l'environnement et l'ecologie sont les maîtres mots, traduits dans la Passivhaus, standard de construction écologique qui vise à créer des maisons très économes en énergie en utilisant des techniques d'isolation et d'étanchéité à l'air avancées. L'entreprise est une référence méditerranéenne non seulement en matière d'architecture et de design, mais aussi dans la promotion du style de vie de Jávea, de l'artisanat local et de la culture.

La firma Jessica Bataille nace de la tienda —Rust&Co— que la diseñadora estableció en 1996, cuando tenía 20 años. En ese momento fue una pionera en transformar muebles de estilo mexicano, con gran éxito. Tras 25 años, la compañía cuenta con nueve empresas y más de 60 profesionales de la arquitectura, el arte, el diseño y la ingeniería. En Jessica Bataille el respeto por el entorno y la sostenibilidad son sellos de identidad, traducidos en las Passivhaus, un estándar de construcción ecológica que tiene como objetivo crear casas de alta eficiencia energética utilizando técnicas avanzadas de aislamiento y sellado del aire. La firma es una referencia mediterránea no sólo en arquitectura y diseño, sino en la promoción del estilo de vida de Jávea, la artesanía local y la cultura.

Mediterranean warmth, global furnishings, and sustainable design converge, reflecting Jessica Bataille's commitment to beauty, well-being, and respect for nature.

CASA ONDAS

An elevated retreat where open spaces, layered roofs, and natural light merge to create a seamless connection between tropical living and breathtaking ocean views.

Placed in a small terrace in the mountains of Playa Tamarindo with amazing ocean views, we found Casa Ondas. It was conceptualized as an elongated structure, positioned in an existent terrace, with two main volumes separated by an open but covered terrace, dividing Social from Private areas. The house was designed in multiple levels for a better use of the existent terrace and sloped areas around it. Four independents and very particular roofs, overlaps on top of the social and private areas, unifying the program of the house and bringing a lot of light in between the roof, creating a unique space for the social areas. Steel columns support the roofs with just a few lower walls, creating very big opening to the views and bringing a lot of natural light into the spaces and the elongated shape of the house improves natural cross ventilation through all the house.
This house was created with the intention of increasing the interaction of the interior and exterior space, so that the user can truly experience life in the tropics.

Située dans les montagnes de Playa Tamarindo, avec une vue imprenable sur la mer, se trouve la Casa Ondas. Elle a été conçue comme une structure allongée, positionnée sur une terrasse existante, avec deux volumes principaux séparés par une terrasse ouverte mais couverte, séparant les zones sociales des zones privées. La maison a été conçue sur plusieurs niveaux afin d'utiliser au mieux la terrasse existante et les zones en pente qui l'entourent. Quatre toits indépendants et très particuliers se chevauchent au sommet, unifiant le programme de la maison et apportant beaucoup de lumière entre les toits, créant un espace unique pour les parties communes. Des colonnes en acier soutiennent les plafonds avec seulement quelques murs en dessous, créant de grandes ouvertures vers les vues et permettant à la lumière naturelle de pénétrer dans les espaces.
La forme allongée de la maison favorise la ventilation transversale naturelle. Cette maison a été créée dans le but d'accroître l'interaction entre l'espace intérieur et l'espace extérieur.

Auf einer kleinen Terrasse in den Bergen von Playa Tamarindo mit herrlichem Blick auf das Meer befindet sich Casa Ondas. Es wurde als langgestreckte Struktur konzipiert, die in einer bestehenden Terrasse positioniert ist, mit zwei Hauptvolumina, die durch eine offene, aber überdachte Terrasse getrennt sind, die den Sozialbereich vom Privatbereich trennt. Das Haus wurde auf mehreren Ebenen entworfen, um die vorhandene Terrasse und die schrägen Bereiche um sie herum besser nutzen zu können. Vier unabhängige und sehr spezielle Dächer, die sich über den sozialen und privaten Bereichen überlappen, vereinen das Programm des Hauses und lassen viel Licht zwischen den Dächern herein, wodurch ein einzigartiger Raum für die sozialen Bereiche entsteht.
Stahlsäulen stützen die Dächer mit nur wenigen niedrigeren Wänden, wodurch eine sehr große Öffnung für die Aussicht geschaffen wird und viel natürliches Licht in die Räume gelangt, und die längliche Form des Hauses verbessert die natürliche Querlüftung im ganzen Haus.

Ubicada en una pequeña terraza en las montañas de Playa Tamarindo con impresionantes vistas al mar, encontramos Casa Ondas. Fue conceptualizada como una estructura alargada, posicionada en una terraza existente, con dos volúmenes principales separados por una terraza abierta pero cubierta, dividiendo las áreas sociales de las privadas. La casa fue diseñada en múltiples niveles para un mejor uso de la terraza existente y las áreas inclinadas que la rodean. Cuatro techos independientes y muy particulares se superponen en la parte superior, unificando el programa de la casa y proporcionando mucha luz entre los techos, creando un espacio único para las áreas comunes. Columnas de acero sostienen los techos con solo unas pocas paredes inferiores, creando grandes aberturas hacia las vistas y permitiendo que mucha luz natural entre en los espacios.
La forma alargada de la casa mejora la ventilación natural cruzada. Esta casa fue creada con la intención de aumentar la interacción entre el espacio interior y exterior.

Photos: © Andres Garcia Lachner

LSD ARCHITECTS

Rodolfo Tinocco, Luis Mauricio Solís

Our office is based in Tamarindo, Guanacaste, Costa Rica. We built our company in 2006. Since then, we have been exploring techniques, materials, environments and disciplines. Our international and local experience gives us a wide perspective when approaching a project. We take enough time to understand and interpret our clients needs and desires. We work hand in hand with our clients, architects, designers, engineers, builders, accountants and environmentalists. We love to introduce new ways of thinking our projects. That's why we call ourselves a "laboratory." We are constantly combining structures, materials and perspectives in the entire process. We prefer local materials, techniques and manpower.

Unser Büro befindet sich in Tamarindo, Guanacaste, Costa Rica. Wir haben unser Unternehmen im Jahr 2006 gegründet. Seitdem haben wir Techniken, Materialien, Umgebungen und Disziplinen erkundet. Unsere internationale und lokale Erfahrung gibt uns eine breite Perspektive, wenn wir ein Projekt angehen. Wir nehmen uns Zeit, um die Bedürfnisse und Wünsche unserer Kunden zu verstehen und zu interpretieren. Wir arbeiten Hand in Hand mit unseren Kunden, Architekten, Designern, Ingenieuren, Bauunternehmern, Wirtschaftsprüfern und Umweltschützern. Wir lieben es, neue Denkansätze in unsere Projekte einzubringen. Deshalb nennen wir uns ein „Labor." Während des gesamten Prozesses kombinieren wir ständig Strukturen, Materialien und Perspektiven. Wir bevorzugen lokale Materialien, Techniken und Verarbeitung.

Notre bureau est situé à Tamarindo, Guanacaste, Costa Rica. Nous avons créé notre entreprise en 2006. Depuis lors, nous avons exploré des techniques, des matériaux, des environnements et des disciplines. Notre expérience internationale et locale nous permet d'avoir une large perspective lorsque nous abordons un projet. Nous prenons le temps de comprendre et d'interpréter les besoins et les désirs de nos clients. Nous travaillons main dans la main avec nos clients, architectes, designers, ingénieurs, constructeurs, comptables et écologistes. Nous aimons introduire de nouvelles façons de penser dans nos projets. C'est pourquoi nous nous qualifions de « laboratoire ». Nous combinons constamment les structures, les matériaux et les perspectives tout au long du processus. Nous préférons les matériaux, les techniques et la main-d'œuvre locaux.

Nuestra oficina se encuentra en Tamarindo, Guanacaste, Costa Rica. Construimos nuestra empresa en 2006. Desde entonces, hemos estado explorando técnicas, materiales, ambientes y disciplinas. Nuestra experiencia internacional y local nos da una amplia perspectiva al abordar un proyecto. Nos tomamos el tiempo suficiente para entender e interpretar las necesidades y deseos de nuestros clientes. Trabajamos mano a mano con nuestros clientes, arquitectos, diseñadores, ingenieros, constructores, contables y ecologistas. Nos encanta introducir nuevas formas de pensar en nuestros proyectos. Por eso nos llamamos «laboratorio». Combinamos constantemente estructuras, materiales y perspectivas en todo el proceso. Preferimos los materiales, las técnicas y la mano de obra locales.

Designed to celebrate Costa Rica's landscape, the house blends terraces, steel structures, and local craftsmanship, encouraging an authentic experience of indoor-outdoor tropical life.

CASA DOS MORES

A harmonious retreat on the cliffs of Portugal, where seamless indoor-outdoor living meets timeless design and artisanal craftsmanship.

An exceptional viewpoint on a cliff, with open views of the ocean and the infinite horizon, but sheltered by lush vegetation. This is the enclave in which this house is located: pure serenity, invaded by the scent of the sea and graced by the sound of birds. The topography offered the rare opportunity to design a house that defies the distinction between inside and outside thanks to the full-height windows, while maintaining a sense of privacy and exclusive seclusion. The use of wood and glass has minimised the impact that typical Portuguese white walls would have created. Inside, the bright spaces are defined by bold elements such as the wooden staircases and bespoke furniture of exceptional craftsmanship. Two large skylights have been placed to maximise the feeling of being immersed in nature, a distinctive motif in the architectural narrative of the house. All spaces are large and open, with a few selected decorative elements defining them and adding character, while allowing the quality and texture of the solid wood and glass to play their full part.

Un point de vue exceptionnel sur une falaise, avec des vues ouvertes sur l'océan et l'horizon infini, mais abrité par une végétation luxuriante. Telle est l'enclave dans laquelle se trouve cette maison : une pure sérénité, envahie par le parfum de la mer et gratifiée du son des oiseaux. La topographie offrait la rare opportunité de concevoir une maison qui défie la distinction entre l'intérieur et l'extérieur grâce aux fenêtres pleine hauteur, tout en maintenant un sentiment d'intimité et d'isolement exclusif. L'utilisation du bois et du verre a minimisé l'impact que les murs blancs typiquement portugais auraient créé. À l'intérieur, les espaces lumineux sont définis par des éléments audacieux tels que les escaliers en bois et le mobilier sur mesure d'une qualité exceptionnelle. Deux grands puits de lumière ont été placés pour maximiser le sentiment d'être immergé dans la nature, un motif distinctif dans le récit architectural de la maison. Tous les espaces sont vastes et ouverts, et quelques éléments décoratifs choisis les définissent et leur donnent du caractère, tout en laissant la qualité et la texture du bois massif et du verre jouer pleinement leur rôle.

Ein außergewöhnlicher Aussichtspunkt auf einer Klippe, mit freiem Blick auf den Ozean und den unendlichen Horizont, aber geschützt durch üppige Vegetation. Das ist die Enklave, in der sich dieses Haus befindet: pure Ruhe, durchdrungen vom Duft des Meeres und begleitet vom Gesang der Vögel. Die Topografie bot die seltene Gelegenheit, ein Haus zu entwerfen, das dank der raumhohen Fenster die Unterscheidung zwischen Innen und Außen aufhebt und gleichzeitig ein Gefühl von Privatsphäre und exklusiver Abgeschiedenheit vermittelt. Durch die Verwendung von Holz und Glas wurde die Wirkung der typisch portugiesischen weißen Wände auf ein Minimum reduziert. Im Inneren werden die hellen Räume durch kühne Elemente wie die Holztreppen und die maßgefertigten Möbel von außergewöhnlicher Handwerkskunst bestimmt. Zwei große Oberlichter wurden angebracht, um das Gefühl, in die Natur eingetaucht zu sein, zu maximieren - ein charakteristisches Motiv in der architektonischen Erzählung des Hauses. Alle Räume sind groß und offen, mit einigen ausgewählten dekorativen Elementen, die sie definieren und ihnen Charakter verleihen, während die Qualität und Textur des Massivholzes und des Glases ihre volle Wirkung entfalten können.

Un mirador excepcional en un acantilado, con vistas al océano y al horizonte infinito, pero resguardado por una exuberante vegetación. Este es el enclave en el que se encuentra esta casa: pura serenidad, invadida por el aroma del mar y agraciada por el sonido de los pájaros. La topografía ofreció la oportunidad, no tan común, de diseñar una casa que desafía la distinción entre el interior y el exterior gracias a las ventanas de altura completa, manteniendo al mismo tiempo la sensación de privacidad y aislamiento exclusivo. El uso de la madera y cristal ha minimizado el impacto que habrían creado las típicas paredes blancas portuguesas. En el interior, los espacios luminosos están definidos por elementos audaces, como las escaleras de madera y el mobiliario hecho a medida de una artesanía excepcional. Se han colocado dos grandes claraboyas para maximizar la sensación de estar inmerso en la naturaleza, un motivo distintivo de la narrativa arquitectónica de la casa. Los espacios son amplios y abiertos, con pocos elementos decorativos seleccionados que los definen y aportan carácter, al tiempo que permiten que la calidad y la textura de la madera maciza y el cristal desempeñen plenamente su papel.

Photos: © Renée Kemps

MARLENE ULDSCHMIDT STUDIO

Marlene Uldschmidt

The studio was born in 2005 as a space of the German architect Marlene Uldschmidt dedicated to art. The firm is characterised by rigorous processes that begin with inspiration from the place, the clients and the story it is called upon to tell. The idea is obtained through classic and innovative design, a careful selection of textures and materials, and exceptional craftsmanship to work out the interiors. Each project is treated as something unique that involves the effort to achieve an original result with a clear author's stamp. For this reason, each new work always begins with a blank piece of paper. His aim is to conceive a solid, high quality project and to transmit reliability and confidence to his clients, whose dreams he sculpts from the raw material with diligence and honesty.

Das Studio wurde 2005 als ein der Kunst gewidmeter Raum der deutschen Architektin Marlene Uldschmidt gegründet. Das Büro zeichnet sich durch rigorose Prozesse aus, die mit der Inspiration durch den Ort, die Kunden und die Geschichte, die es zu erzählen hat, beginnen. Die Idee wird durch klassisches und innovatives Design, eine sorgfältige Auswahl von Texturen und Materialien sowie außergewöhnliche Handwerkskunst bei der Realisierung der Innenräume umgesetzt. Jedes Projekt wird als etwas Einzigartiges behandelt, bei dem es darum geht, ein originelles Ergebnis zu erzielen, das eindeutig die Handschrift des Autors trägt. Deshalb beginnt jede neue Arbeit immer mit einem leeren Blatt Papier. Sein Ziel ist es, ein solides, qualitativ hochwertiges Projekt zu konzipieren und seinen Kunden, deren Träume er mit Strenge und Ehrlichkeit aus dem Rohmaterial formt, Zuverlässigkeit und Vertrauen zu vermitteln.

Le studio est né en 2005 comme un espace de l'architecte allemande Marlene Uldschmidt dédié à l'art. Le cabinet se caractérise par des processus rigoureux qui commencent par s'inspirer du lieu, des clients et de l'histoire qu'il est appelé à raconter. Cette idée se concrétise par un design classique et innovant, une sélection minutieuse des textures et des matériaux, et un savoir-faire exceptionnel pour la réalisation des intérieurs. Chaque projet est traité comme quelque chose d'unique qui implique l'effort d'atteindre un résultat original avec une empreinte claire de l'auteur. C'est pourquoi chaque nouvelle œuvre commence toujours par une feuille de papier vierge. Son objectif est de concevoir un projet solide et de qualité et de transmettre fiabilité et confiance à ses clients, dont il sculpte les rêves à partir de la matière première avec rigueur et honnêteté.

El estudio nació en 2005 como un espacio de la arquitecta alemana Marlene Uldschmidt dedicado al arte. La firma se caracteriza por llevar a cabo procesos rigurosos que comienzan con la inspiración a partir del lugar, los clientes y la historia que está llamada a contar. La idea se materializa a través del diseño clásico e innovador, una cuidadosa selección de texturas y materiales, y una artesanía excepcional para realizar los interiores. Cada proyecto se trata como algo único que conlleva el esfuerzo por conseguir un resultado original con un claro sello de autor. Por eso, cada nuevo trabajo comienza siempre con un papel en blanco. Su propósito de concebir un proyecto sólido, de gran calidad, y transmitir fiabilidad y confianza a sus clientes, cuyos sueños esculpe de la materia prima con rigor y honestidad.

Hong Kong, China.

THE IMPERFECT RESIDENCE

Embracing the timeless philosophy of wabi sabi, this Hong Kong home blends refined geometry with natural materials for an uncluttered, elegant lifestyle.

Nelson Chow was commissioned to design a new home in Hong Kong for some lifelong friends of his. The clients gave him complete freedom with only three conditions: that it be beautiful, functional and age well. Chow came up with a concept with a visually uncluttered design that meets all the conditions. All the elements appear well integrated as part of the architecture and not as separate, scattered objects. The proposed idea goes beyond the visual and is based on the ancient Japanese philosophy of wabi sabi, which embraces imperfect, impermanent and incomplete beauty. This attitude is the basis of the language that NCDA has translated into a contemporary aesthetic that blends bold geometries with materials in their natural, unfinished state. The house is divided into three zones. The entrance hall and the living room that resembles a sculpture garden. Here folding panels inspired by Shoji screens conceal the storage units. From there it is on to the bedroom, which emerges on a raised platform and where leather and marble reign supreme. The route ends in the dressing room that merges with the bathroom, providing an uninterrupted and fluid ambience that facilitates relaxation.

Nelson Chow a été chargé de concevoir une nouvelle maison à Hong Kong pour certains de ses amis de longue date. Les clients lui ont donné une liberté totale avec seulement trois conditions : qu'il soit beau, fonctionnel et qu'il vieillisse bien. Chow a proposé un concept au design visuellement épuré qui remplit toutes les conditions. L'idée proposée va au-delà du visuel et se fonde sur l'ancienne philosophie japonaise du wabi sabi, qui embrasse la beauté imparfaite, impermanente et incomplète. Cette attitude est la base du langage que NCDA a traduit en une esthétique contemporaine qui mêle des géométries audacieuses à des matériaux dans leur état naturel et non fini. La maison est divisée en trois zones. Le hall d'entrée et le salon qui ressemble à un jardin de sculptures. Ici, des panneaux pliants inspirés des paravents Shoji dissimulent les unités de rangement. De là, on passe à la chambre à coucher, qui émerge sur une plate-forme surélevée et où le cuir et le marbre règnent en maîtres. Le parcours se termine par le dressing qui fusionne avec la salle de bains, offrant une ambiance ininterrompue et fluide qui facilite la relaxation.

Nelson Chow wurde beauftragt, ein neues Haus in Hongkong für einige seiner lebenslangen Freunde zu entwerfen. Die Kunden ließen ihm völlige Freiheit mit nur drei Bedingungen: Es sollte schön und funktionell sein und gut altern. Chow entwickelte ein Konzept mit einem visuell aufgeräumten Design, das alle Bedingungen erfüllt. Die vorgeschlagene Idee geht über das Visuelle hinaus und basiert auf der alten japanischen Philosophie des wabi sabi, die unvollkommene, unbeständige und unvollständige Schönheit anerkennt. Diese Haltung ist die Grundlage für die Sprache, die NCDA in eine zeitgenössische Ästhetik übersetzt hat, die kühne Geometrien mit Materialien in ihrem natürlichen, unbearbeiteten Zustand verbindet. Das Haus ist in drei Bereiche unterteilt. Die Eingangshalle und das Wohnzimmer, das an einen Skulpturengarten erinnert. Hier verbergen von Shoji-Schirmen inspirierte Faltpaneele die Schränke. Von dort aus geht es weiter zum Schlafzimmer, das auf einem erhöhten Podest liegt und in dem Leder und Marmor die Oberhand haben. Die Reise endet in der Umkleidekabine, die mit dem Badezimmer verschmilzt und eine ununterbrochene und fließende Umgebung bietet, die die Entspannung fördert.

Nelson Chow recibió el encargo de diseñar la nueva casa en Hong Kong de unos amigos suyos de toda la vida. Los clientes le dieron total libertad con sólo tres condiciones: que fuera bonita, funcional y que envejeciera bien. Chow propuso un concepto con un diseño visualmente despejado y que cumple todas las condiciones. La idea propuesta va más allá de lo visual y se basa en la antigua filosofía japonesa del wabi sabi, que abraza la belleza imperfecta, impermanente e incompleta. Esta actitud es la base del lenguaje que NCDA ha traducido en una estética contemporánea que mezcla geometrías atrevidas con materiales en su estado natural inacabado. La casa se divide en tres zonas. El vestíbulo y la sala de estar que parece un jardín de esculturas. Aquí los paneles plegables inspirados en los biombos Shoji ocultan las unidades de almacenamiento. De allí se pasa al dormitorio que emerge sobre una plataforma elevada y donde impera la piel y el mármol. El trayecto termina en el vestidor que se funde con el cuarto de baño, proporcionando un ambiente ininterrumpido y fluido y facilitando la relajación.

Photos: © Harold De Puymorin

NC DESIGN & ARCHITECTURE

Nelson Chow

Nelson Chow is renowned for his designs of residential, commercial and hospitality projects with a soft, tactile and welcoming aesthetic. He studied architecture at the University of Waterloo and tailoring at the Fashion Institute of Technology in New York. He began his career at the renowned AvroKO studio, before moving back to Hong Kong, where he set up NCDA in 2011. Chow first came to prominence in 2016 when his elegant and sophisticated interior design for Foxglove, won the London Restaurant and Bar Design Award for Best Bar in Asia. Since then, the studio has worked for blue-chip international clients. NCDA takes a holistic approach where everything - from the interior, furniture, lighting and graphic design - is customised to create unique narratives.

Nelson Chow ist bekannt für seine Entwürfe für Wohn-, Geschäfts- und Gaststättenprojekte mit einer weichen, taktilen und einladenden Ästhetik. Er studierte Architektur an der University of Waterloo und Schneiderei am Fashion Institute of Technology in New York. Er begann seine Karriere im renommierten Studio AvroKO, bevor er nach Hongkong zurückkehrte, wo er 2011 NCDA gründete. Chow wurde erstmals 2016 bekannt, als sein elegantes und anspruchsvolles Innendesign für das Foxglove mit dem London Restaurant and Bar Design Award für die beste Bar in Asien ausgezeichnet wurde. Seitdem hat das Studio für erstklassige internationale Kunden gearbeitet. NCDA verfolgt einen ganzheitlichen Ansatz, bei dem alles - von der Inneneinrichtung über die Möbel und die Beleuchtung bis hin zum Grafikdesign - individuell gestaltet wird, um einzigartige Geschichten zu schaffen.

Nelson Chow est réputé pour ses conceptions de projets résidentiels, commerciaux et d'accueil à l'esthétique douce, tactile et accueillante. Il a étudié l'architecture à l'université de Waterloo et la couture au Fashion Institute of Technology de New York. Il a commencé sa carrière au célèbre studio AvroKO, avant de revenir à Hong Kong, où il a créé NCDA en 2011. Chow s'est fait connaître pour la première fois en 2016 lorsque sa décoration intérieure élégante et sophistiquée pour Foxglove, a remporté le London Restaurant and Bar Design Award du meilleur bar en Asie. Depuis lors, le studio a travaillé pour des clients internationaux de premier ordre. NCDA adopte une approche holistique où tout – de l'intérieur, du mobilier, de l'éclairage et du design graphique - est personnalisé pour créer des récits uniques.

Nelson Chow es famoso por sus diseños de proyectos residenciales, comerciales y de hostelería, con una estética suave, táctil y acogedora. Estudió arquitectura en la Universidad de Waterloo, y sastrería en el Fashion Institute of Technology de Nueva York. Comenzó su carrera en el renombrado estudio AvroKO, antes de trasladarse de nuevo a Hong Kong, donde creó NCDA en 2011. Chow se dio a conocer en 2016 cuando su elegante y sofisticado interiorismo para Foxglove, ganó el Premio de Diseño de Restaurantes y Bares de Londres como mejor bar de Asia. Desde entonces, el estudio ha trabajado para clientes internacionales de primer orden. NCDA tiene un enfoque holístico donde todo —desde el interior, el mobiliario, la iluminación y el diseño gráfico— se personaliza para crear narrativas únicas.

Folding Shoji-style panels, a raised platform, and seamless transitions highlight NCDA's creative use of space and their innovative interpretation of wabi sabi.

Austin, Texas, United States

THE PERCH

Gently perched above the bungalow, this minimalist studio maintains harmony with the surrounding landscape while providing an efficient, light-filled living space.

The Perch is a 61.32 m² studio shaped to fit above the existing bungalow roofline and just below the City of Austin setback tent limiting building height. Owners Annie and Dylan, a hairstylist and a landscape designer, wanted to keep their backyard intact, not move during construction, nor disrupt the mature landscape. The Perch rests on four steel columns, three of which pierce through existing bungalow walls to resist lateral forces. Shop-built steel framing was craned into place to minimally disturb the site. The cantilevered form gently sways in the wind, a reminder of its construction. Materials were selected for durability, economy, and serenity including whitewashed pine walls and ceilings (spanning from the exterior porch into the interior), maple butcher block countertops, and white oak flooring throughout.

The Perch est un studio de 61,32 m² conçu pour s'adapter au-dessus de la ligne de toit du bungalow existant et juste en dessous de la limite de hauteur de construction de la ville d'Austin. Les propriétaires, Annie et Dylan, une styliste et un paysagiste, voulaient préserver leur arrière-cour, ne pas déménager pendant la construction et ne pas perturber le paysage. The Perch repose sur quatre colonnes en acier, dont trois traversent les murs existants pour résister aux forces latérales. Le cadre en acier construit en atelier a été placé avec une grue pour perturber le moins possible l'endroit. La forme en porte-à-faux se balance doucement dans le vent, rappelant sa construction. Les matériaux ont été sélectionnés pour leur durabilité et leur économie, notamment des murs et des plafonds en pin blanchi (s'étendant de la véranda extérieure à l'intérieur), des plans de travail en blocs d'érable et des sols en chêne blanc dans tout l'espace.

The Perch ist ein 61,32 m² großes Studio, das so konzipiert wurde, dass es über der Dachlinie des vorhandenen Bungalows liegt und knapp unter der Höhenbegrenzung der Stadt Austin bleibt. Die Besitzer, Annie und Dylan, eine Stylistin und ein Landschaftsgestalter, wollten ihren Hinterhof intakt halten, während der Bau stattfand, und die Landschaft nicht stören. The Perch ruht auf vier Stahlsäulen, von denen drei die bestehenden Wände durchdringen, um seitliche Kräfte zu widerstehen. Der im Werk gebaute Stahlrahmen wurde mit einem Kran minimalinvasiv am Ort platziert. Die auskragende Form schaukelt sanft im Wind und erinnert an ihre Konstruktion. Die Materialien wurden aufgrund ihrer Haltbarkeit und Wirtschaftlichkeit ausgewählt, einschließlich gekalkter Kiefernwände und Decken (die vom äußeren Vordach bis ins Innere reichen), Ahornblock-Arbeitsplatten und weiße Eicheböden im gesamten Raum.

The Perch es un estudio de 61,32 m² diseñado para adaptarse por encima de la línea del techo del bungalow existente y justo debajo de la linea de la Ciudad de Austin que limita la altura de construcción. Los propietarios, Annie y Dylan, una estilista y un paisajista, querían mantener intacto su patio trasero, no mudarse durante la construcción ni perturbar el paisaje. The Perch descansa sobre cuatro columnas de acero, tres de las cuales atraviesan las paredes existentes para resistir las fuerzas laterales. El armazón de acero construido en taller se colocó con grúa para perturbar mínimamente el lugar. La forma en voladizo se balancea suavemente en el viento, recordando su construcción. Los materiales fueron seleccionados por su durabilidad y economía, incluyendo paredes y techos de pino encalado (que se extienden desde el porche exterior hasta el interior), encimeras de bloques de arce y pisos de roble blanco en todo el espacio.

Photos: © Casey Dunn

PATTERNS of INDIA
URBAN JUNGLE
CUTTING HAIR THE VIDAL SASSOON WAY

NICOLE BLAIR

Nicole Blair

Nicole Blair is an architect and general contractor working in Austin, Texas, the city where she was born and raised. Her practice focuses on residential, small commercial, and public art building projects. In 2019 Elle Decor named Nicole one of the greatest living architects in the world, alongside several Pritzker Prize winners. Her projects have received numerous design awards – local to international – and her work has been published in books, magazines, and ad campaigns worldwide. She gained early work experience in the NYC offices of Robert A.M. Stern and Peter Eisenman architects and obtained a Bachelor of Science in Textiles and Apparel from Cornell and a Master of Architecture from Rice.

Nicole Blair ist eine Architektin und Generalunternehmerin, die in Austin, Texas, arbeitet, der Stadt, in der sie geboren und aufgewachsen ist. Ihr Fokus liegt auf Wohnbau, kleinen Gewerbeimmobilien und öffentlicher Kunst. 2019 ernannte Elle Decor Nicole zu einer der bedeutendsten lebenden Architektinnen der Welt, neben mehreren Pritzker-Preisträgern. Ihre Projekte wurden mit zahlreichen Designpreisen, sowohl lokal als auch international, ausgezeichnet, und ihre Arbeit wurde in Büchern, Zeitschriften und Werbekampagnen auf der ganzen Welt veröffentlicht. Sie sammelte frühzeitig Berufserfahrung in den New Yorker Büros der Architekten Robert A.M. Stern und Peter Eisenman und erwarb einen Bachelor of Science in Textilien und Bekleidung an der Cornell University sowie einen Master in Architektur an der Rice University.

Nicole Blair est une architecte et entrepreneuse générale travaillant à Austin, au Texas, la ville où elle est née et a grandi. Son studio se concentre sur des projets de construction résidentielle, de petits commerces et d'art public. En 2019, Elle Decor a nommé Nicole l'une des plus grandes architectes vivantes au monde, aux côtés de plusieurs lauréats du Prix Pritzker. Ses projets ont reçu de nombreux prix de design, tant locaux qu'internationaux, et son travail a été publié dans des livres, des magazines et des campagnes publicitaires à travers le monde. Elle a acquis une expérience professionnelle précoce dans les bureaux new-yorkais des architectes Robert A.M. Stern et Peter Eisenman, et a obtenu un baccalauréat ès sciences en textiles et confection de l'Université Cornell et une maîtrise en architecture de l'Université Rice.

Nicole Blair es una arquitecta y contratista general que trabaja en Austin, Texas, la ciudad donde nació y creció. Su estudio se centra en proyectos de construcción residencial, pequeños comercios y arte público. En 2019, Elle Decor nombró a Nicole una de las mayores arquitectas vivas del mundo, junto con varios ganadores del Premio Pritzker. Sus proyectos han recibido numerosos premios de diseño, tanto locales como internacionales, y su trabajo ha sido publicado en libros, revistas y campañas publicitarias en todo el mundo. Obtuvo experiencia laboral temprana en las oficinas de Nueva York de los arquitectos Robert A.M. Stern y Peter Eisenman, y obtuvo una Licenciatura en Ciencias en Textiles y Confección de la Universidad de Cornell y una Maestría en Arquitectura de Rice.

JUNGALOW

FISHER & PAYKEL

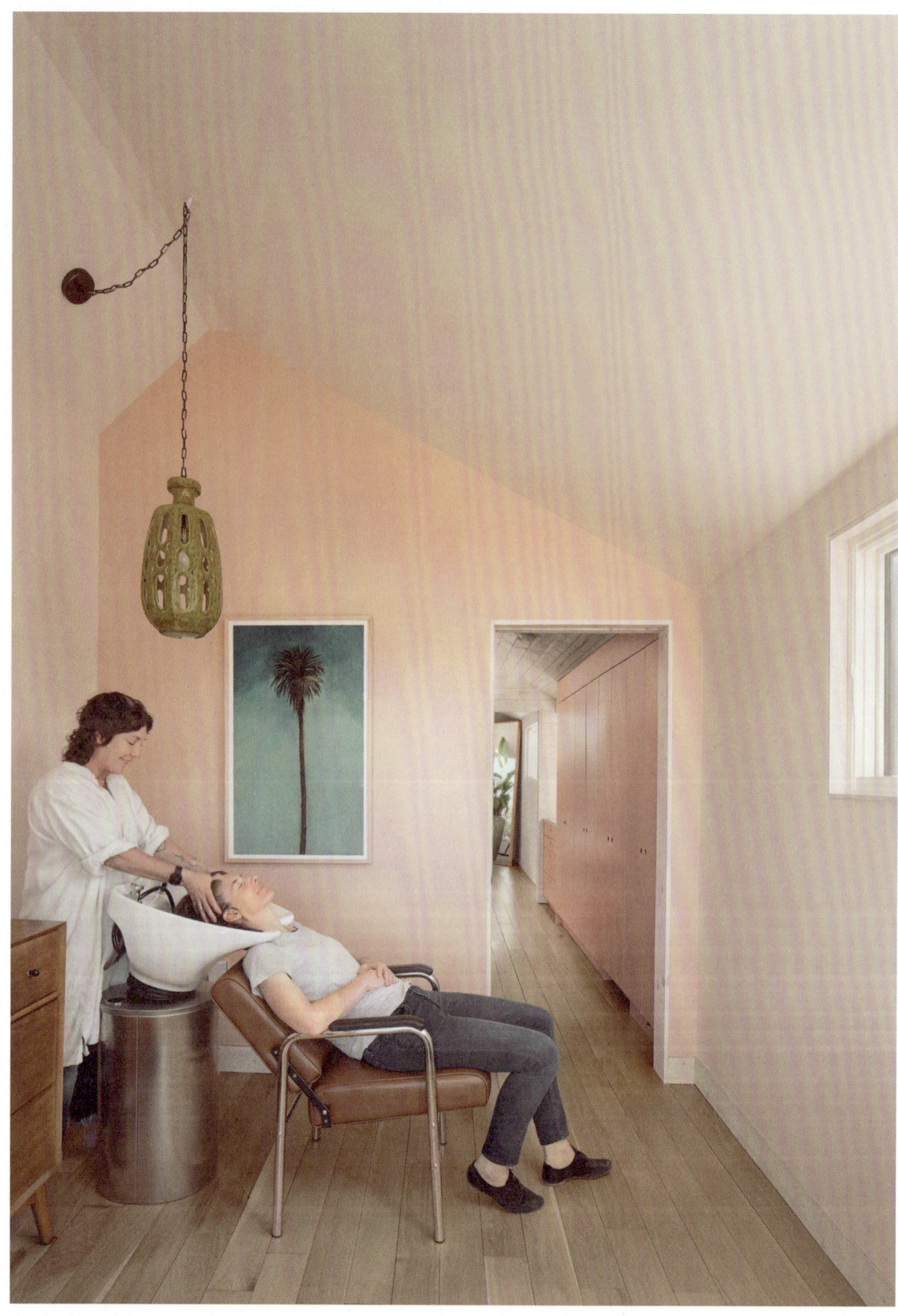

Durable materials and a thoughtful layout define Nicole Blair's vision, where practicality and serenity merge effortlessly in a compact Austin studio.

1621

Hod Hasharon, Israel

MO HOUSE

Wood, natural fibers, and soft tones imbue this renovated home with warmth, light, and a soothing sense of calm.

This house is the result of a complete renovation that brought light and warmth to all the rooms, but above all a sense of calm. The large outdoor garden with fruit trees is accessed through the patio doors adjacent to the main area. The living room is dominated by a combination of wood and metal, which is repeated in the coffee tables and the light fixtures on the ceiling rail. The leather chairs have a wooden frame and the fabric chairs are made of metal. A large central sofa in ecru combines with wool and natural fibre textiles to create an organic look. The parquet floor is of natural oak and has replaced the old one, giving a pleasant homely feel. The dining room and kitchen maintain the same chromatic range, giving priority to textures and matching details such as the hanging lamps. The suite is located in the attic, which has been divided into different areas to make the most of the space. A glass wall with different degrees of transparency separates the bathroom from the sleeping area. White dominates the furnishings and finishes such as porcelain tiles, interrupted only by the oak floor and the veins of the marble.

Cette maison est le résultat d'une rénovation complète qui a apporté lumière et chaleur à toutes les pièces, mais surtout un sentiment de calme. Le grand jardin extérieur avec des arbres fruitiers est accessible par les portes-fenêtres adjacentes à la zone principale. Le salon est dominé par une combinaison de bois et de métal, qui se retrouve dans les tables basses et les luminaires du rail de plafond. Les chaises en cuir ont une structure en bois et les chaises en tissu sont en métal. Un grand canapé central en écru se combine avec des textiles en laine et en fibres naturelles pour créer un look organique. Le parquet est en chêne naturel et a remplacé l'ancien, ce qui donne une agréable sensation de confort. La salle à manger et la cuisine conservent la même gamme chromatique, en privilégiant les textures et les détails assortis, comme les lampes suspendues. La suite est située dans le grenier, qui a été divisé en différentes zones pour tirer le meilleur parti de l'espace. Une paroi en verre avec différents degrés de transparence sépare la salle de bains de la zone de couchage. Le blanc domine l'ameublement et les finitions telles que les carreaux de porcelaine, interrompus seulement par le plancher en chêne et les veines du marbre.

Dieses Haus ist das Ergebnis einer kompletten Renovierung, die allen Räumen Licht und Wärme, vor allem aber ein Gefühl der Ruhe verliehen hat. Der große Garten mit Obstbäumen ist durch die Terrassentüren neben dem Hauptraum zugänglich. Das Wohnzimmer wird von einer Kombination aus Holz und Metall dominiert, die sich in den Couchtischen und den Leuchten an der Deckenschiene wiederfindet. Die Lederstühle haben einen Holzrahmen und die Stoffstühle sind aus Metall. Ein großes zentrales Sofa in Ecru kombiniert mit Textilien aus Wolle und Naturfasern sorgt für einen organischen Look. Der Parkettboden ist aus natürlicher Eiche und hat den alten Fußboden ersetzt, was ein angenehmes Wohngefühl vermittelt. Im Esszimmer und in der Küche wird die gleiche Farbpalette beibehalten, wobei Texturen und passende Details wie die Hängelampen im Vordergrund stehen. Die Suite befindet sich im Dachgeschoss, das in verschiedene Bereiche unterteilt wurde, um den Raum optimal zu nutzen. Eine Glaswand mit unterschiedlichen Transparenzgraden trennt das Bad vom Schlafbereich. Weiß dominiert das Mobiliar und die Oberflächen, wie z. B. die Porzellanfliesen, die nur durch den Eichenboden und die Maserung des Marmors unterbrochen werden.

Esta casa es el resultado de una reforma integral que aportó luminosidad y calidez a todos los ambientes, pero sobre todo una sensación de calma. El amplio jardín exterior con árboles frutales se cuela por las puertas del patio adyacente a la zona principal. En el salón predomina una combinación de madera y metal que se repite en las mesas de centro y en los apliques de luz en el riel del techo. Las sillas de cuero tienen estructura de madera, y las de tela, de metal. Un gran sofá central de color crudo, combina con textiles de lana y fibras naturales para crear un aspecto orgánico. El suelo de parquet es de roble natural y ha sustituido al antiguo aportando un agradable aire hogareño. El comedor y la cocina mantienen la misma gama cromática dando prioridad a las texturas y los detalles a juego como las lámparas colgantes. La suite se encuentra en el ático que se ha dividido en distintas zonas para aprovechar el espacio. Una pared de cristal con distintos grados de transparencia separa el cuarto de baño de la zona de dormitorio. El blanco impera en el mobiliario y los acabados como los azulejos de porcelana, y se interrumpe sólo con el suelo de roble y las vetas del mármol.

Photos: © Gilad Redt

ODELIA BARZILAY INTERIOR DESIGN

Odelia Barzilay

Designer, creator, entrepreneur, artist and writer, Odelia Barzilay is the head of the boutique architecture and interior design studio that bears her name. With a career spanning 18 years in the industry, she has worked alongside leading figures in the design and planning of homes of the highest quality standards. Her talent for understanding her clients' needs results in tailor-made projects that make their dreams come true, with professionalism and creativity. The work of the studio is inspired by modern design trends and innovative materials, with a focus on client comfort and quality of life.

Odelia Barzilay, Designerin, Unternehmerin, Künstlerin und Schriftstellerin, ist die Leiterin des Architektur- und Innenarchitekturbüros, das ihren Namen trägt. In ihrer 18-jährigen Karriere in der Branche hat sie mit führenden Persönlichkeiten bei der Gestaltung und Planung von Häusern mit höchsten Qualitätsstandards zusammengearbeitet. Sein Talent, die Bedürfnisse seiner Kunden zu verstehen, führt zu maßgeschneiderten Projekten, die ihre Träume mit Professionalität und Kreativität wahr werden lassen. Ihre Arbeit wird von modernen Designtrends und innovativen Materialien inspiriert, wobei der Komfort und die Lebensqualität der Kunden im Mittelpunkt stehen.

Designer, créatrice, entrepreneuse, artiste et écrivain, Odelia Barzilay est à la tête du studio d'architecture et de décoration intérieure qui porte son nom. Avec une carrière de 18 ans dans le secteur, elle a travaillé aux côtés de personnalités de premier plan dans la conception et la planification de logements répondant aux normes de qualité les plus élevées. Son talent pour comprendre les besoins de ses clients se traduit par des projets sur mesure qui font de leurs rêves une réalité, avec professionnalisme et créativité. Le travail de l'étude s'inspire des tendances du design moderne et des matériaux innovants, en mettant l'accent sur le confort et la qualité de vie des clients.

Diseñadora, creadora, empresaria, artista y escritora, Odelia Barzilay está al frente del estudio boutique de arquitectura y diseño de interiores que lleva su nombre. Con una trayectoria de 18 años en el sector, ha trabajado junto a figuras destacadas del diseño y la planificación de viviendas con los más altos estándares de calidad. Su talento para entender las necesidades de sus clientes, resulta en proyectos a medida que hacen realidad sus sueños, con profesionalidad y creatividad. Su trabajo se inspira en las tendencias del diseño moderno y los materiales innovadores, con un enfoque centrado en la comodidad del cliente y su calidad de vida.

A blend of textures and a serene palette reflect Odelia Barzilay's dedication to creating personalized, harmonious spaces that inspire comfort and tranquility.

V AND L CABIN

Blending solid timber construction with sweeping views, these hillside cabins offer a serene, breathable retreat in the Norwegian landscape.

The V and L cabins, designed for two pairs of friends, perch atop a hillside overlooking Lake Krøderen in Norefjell, Norway. True to their names, the cabins consist of two adjacent volumes: one housing the bedrooms and the other featuring an open living and dining area. Notably, the living room is situated a few steps lower than the kitchen, creating a natural division between the spaces. Expansive windows in the living room face eastward, framing the captivating view of the valley below. In the evenings, the two fireplaces take center stage as the main focal points. Both cabins are constructed using solid masstimber, with wooden elements showcased prominently in the interior. The lightly treated walls and ceilings contribute to a breathable and healthy environment. On the exterior, ore pine cladding characterizes the cabins, complemented by contrasting accents in shades of dark red and dark green.

Les cabanes V et L, conçues pour deux couples d'amis, perchent au sommet d'une colline surplombant le lac Krøderen à Norefjell, en Norvège. Fidèles à leurs noms, les cabanes se composent de deux volumes adjacents : l'un abritant les chambres et l'autre proposant un espace de vie et de salle à manger ouvert. Notamment, le salon est situé quelques marches plus bas que la cuisine, créant une division naturelle entre les espaces. Les grandes fenêtres du salon donnent à l'est, encadrant la vue captivante sur la vallée en dessous. Le soir, les deux cheminées deviennent les points focaux principaux. Les deux cabanes sont construites en bois massif, avec des éléments en bois mis en valeur dans l'intérieur. Les murs et plafonds légèrement traités contribuent à un environnement respirant et sain. À l'extérieur, le revêtement en pin ore caractérise les cabanes, complété par des accents contrastés dans des teintes de rouge foncé et de vert foncé.

Die für zwei befreundete Paare konzipierten Hütten V und L liegen auf einem Hügel mit Blick auf den See Krøderen in Norefjell, Norwegen. Wie ihr Name schon sagt, bestehen die Hütten aus zwei nebeneinander liegenden Volumen: in einem befinden sich die Schlafzimmer, im anderen ein offener Wohn- und Essbereich. Das Wohnzimmer liegt ein paar Stufen tiefer als die Küche und schafft so eine natürliche Trennung zwischen den beiden Räumen. Die großen Fenster des Wohnzimmers sind nach Osten ausgerichtet und geben den Blick auf das darunter liegende Tal frei. In den Abendstunden sind die beiden Kamine der Mittelpunkt des Geschehens. Beide Hütten sind aus massivem Massivholz gebaut, wobei die Holzelemente im Innenraum besonders hervorgehoben werden. Die leicht behandelten Wände und Decken tragen zu einer atmungsaktiven und gesunden Umgebung bei. Außen sind die Hütten mit Erzkiefer verkleidet, die durch kontrastierende Akzente in Dunkelrot und Dunkelgrün ergänzt wird.

Las cabañas V y L, diseñadas para dos parejas de amigos, están situadas en lo alto de una colina con vistas al lago Krøderen, en Norefjell (Noruega). Fieles a su nombre, las cabañas constan de dos volúmenes adyacentes: uno alberga los dormitorios y el otro presenta una zona de estar y comedor abierta. El salón está situado unos escalones más abajo que la cocina, lo que crea una división natural entre los espacios. Los amplios ventanales del salón miran hacia el este, enmarcando la cautivadora vista del valle. Por la noche, las dos chimeneas se convierten en el centro de atención. Ambas cabañas están construidas con madera maciza, y los elementos de madera ocupan un lugar destacado en el interior. Las paredes y los techos ligeramente tratados contribuyen a crear un ambiente saludable. En el exterior, el revestimiento de pino mineral caracteriza las cabañas, complementado por acentos de contraste en tonos rojo y verde oscuro.

Photos: © Kyrre Sundal

OSLOTRE

Oslotre Team

Oslotre has been working uniquely with timber architecture and modern timber constructions for more than a decade, serving as an active and innovative driver for transformation in the building industry. Oslotre is a vision-driven office with an interdisciplinary team of architects, engineers, and carpenters who possess one of Europe's foremost expertise in timber architecture. With this unique team, Oslotre can offer a broad portfolio of innovative, biologically based buildings grounded in distinct architectural expertise in timber construction. Oslotre's goal is to contribute to a reduction in greenhouse gas emissions while enhancing the quality of our built environment and spaces.

Oslotre arbeitet seit mehr als einem Jahrzehnt auf einzigartige Weise mit Holzarchitektur und modernen Holzkonstruktionen und ist ein aktiver und innovativer Motor für den Wandel in der Baubranche. Oslotre ist ein visionäres Büro mit einem interdisziplinären Team aus Architekten, Ingenieuren und Zimmerleuten, das in Europa über eines der größten Fachwissen in der Holzarchitektur verfügt. Mit diesem einzigartigen Team kann Oslotre ein breites Portfolio an innovativen, biologisch basierten Gebäuden anbieten, die auf einer ausgeprägten architektonischen Expertise im Holzbau basieren. Das Ziel von Oslotre ist es, zur Reduzierung der Treibhausgasemissionen beizutragen und gleichzeitig die Qualität unserer gebauten Umwelt und unserer Räume zu verbessern.

Oslotre travaille de manière unique dans l'architecture en bois et les constructions modernes en bois depuis plus d'une décennie, en tant que moteur actif et innovant de la transformation de l'industrie du bâtiment. Oslotre est un bureau axé sur la vision avec une équipe interdisciplinaire d'architectes, d'ingénieurs et de charpentiers possédant l'une des expertises les plus importantes d'Europe en architecture en bois. Avec cette équipe unique, Oslotre peut proposer un large portefeuille de bâtiments innovants et biologiquement basés, ancrés dans une expertise architecturale distincte en construction bois. L'objectif d'Oslotre est de contribuer à une réduction des émissions de gaz à effet de serre tout en améliorant la qualité de notre environnement construit et de nos espaces.

Oslotre lleva más de una década trabajando de forma única con la arquitectura de madera y las construcciones modernas de madera, actuando como motor activo e innovador de la transformación en el sector de la construcción. Oslotre es una oficina visionaria que cuenta con un equipo interdisciplinar de arquitectos, ingenieros y carpinteros que poseen una de las mayores competencias de Europa en arquitectura de madera. Con este equipo único, Oslotre puede ofrecer una amplia cartera de edificios innovadores de base biológica basados en una experiencia arquitectónica distintiva en la construcción en madera. El objetivo de Oslotre es contribuir a la reducción de las emisiones de gases de efecto invernadero, mejorando al mismo tiempo la calidad de nuestro entorno y espacios construidos.

Natural wood interiors and carefully placed windows highlight Oslotre's dedication to creating healthy, sustainable living spaces in harmony with the environment.

Bathurst, New Brunswick, Canada

THE SANDBOX

This cedar-clad retreat harmonizes with its harsh coastal surroundings, offering stunning views and enduring craftsmanship that celebrates New Brunswick's rugged beauty.

Inspired by the rugged beauty found in Bathurst, New Brunswick, architect Peter Braithwaite aspired to realize a dwelling that could withstand harsh coastal weather. During the initial site visit, the design team was confronted with horizontal rain and harsh winds that solidified the environmental factors that would drive the design process. The resulting home celebrates a connection to the natural environment and reinforces the importance of resilience. Named "The Sandbox," this cedar- clad home overlooks Chaleur Bay and offers expansive views down the beach and out to the open ocean. The design features generous windows and a rooftop patio accessed by an exterior, weathering steel staircase. Constructed with local building materials and techniques, The Sandbox stands as a testament to community collaboration and enduring craftsmanship, while offering its occupants a retreat that celebrates both the rugged beauty as well as the charm of New Brunswick.

Inspiriert von der rauen Schönheit von Bathurst, New Brunswick, wollte der Architekt Peter Braithwaite ein Haus bauen, das dem rauen Wetter an der Küste standhalten kann. Bei einem ersten Besuch vor Ort wurde das Planungsteam mit horizontalem Regen und heftigen Winden konfrontiert, was die Umweltfaktoren, die den Entwurfsprozess bestimmen sollten, verfestigte. Das entstandene Haus zelebriert die Verbindung zur natürlichen Umgebung und unterstreicht die Bedeutung der Widerstandsfähigkeit. Das mit Zedernholz verkleidete Haus mit dem Namen „The Sandbox" überblickt die Chaleur Bay und bietet einen weiten Blick auf den Strand und das offene Meer. Das Haus ist mit großzügigen Fenstern und einer Dachterrasse ausgestattet, die über eine Außentreppe aus verwittertem Stahl erreichbar ist. Gleichzeitig bietet es seinen Bewohnern einen Rückzugsort, der sowohl die raue Schönheit als auch den Charme von New Brunswick zelebriert.

Inspiré par la beauté sauvage de Bathurst, au Nouveau-Brunswick, l'architecte Peter Braithwaite a aspiré à réaliser une demeure capable de résister aux conditions météorologiques côtières difficiles. Lors de la visite initiale du site, l'équipe de conception a été confrontée à une pluie horizontale et à des vents violents qui ont solidifié les facteurs environnementaux qui allaient guider le processus de conception. La maison résultante célèbre une connexion avec l'environnement naturel et renforce l'importance de la résilience. Nommé « The Sandbox », cette maison revêtue de cèdre surplombe la baie des Chaleurs et offre une vue imprenable sur la plage et sur l'océan ouvert. Le design présente de généreuses fenêtres et un patio sur le toit accessible par un escalier extérieur en acier météorisé. The Sandbox est le témoignage d'une collaboration communautaire et d'un artisanat durable, tout en offrant à ses occupants un refuge qui célèbre à la fois la beauté sauvage et le charme du Nouveau-Brunswick.

Inspirado por la belleza agreste de Bathurst (Nuevo Brunswick), el arquitecto Peter Braithwaite aspiraba a realizar una vivienda que pudiera soportar las duras condiciones climáticas de la costa. Durante la visita inicial al emplazamiento, el equipo de diseño se enfrentó a lluvias horizontales y fuertes vientos que consolidaron los factores medioambientales que impulsarían el proceso de diseño. La casa resultante celebra la conexión con el entorno natural y refuerza la importancia de la resistencia. Bautizada como «The Sandbox», esta casa revestida de cedro se asoma a la bahía de Chaleur y ofrece amplias vistas de la playa y el océano abierto. El diseño presenta amplios ventanales y un patio en la azotea al que se accede por una escalera exterior de acero resistente a la intemperie. Construida con materiales y técnicas de construcción locales, The Sandbox es un testimonio de colaboración comunitaria y artesanía duradera, al tiempo que ofrece a sus ocupantes un refugio que celebra tanto la belleza agreste como el encanto de Nueva Brunswick.

Photos: © Ema Peter

PETER BRAITHWAITE STUDIO

Peter Braithwaite

Peter Braithwaite established Peter Braithwaite Studio Ltd. in 2014 out of a desire to create a company that encompassed both design and construction. Since its establishment the company has completed many interesting residential and commercial projects, and has excelled in cabinetry and furniture design. Our dedication to design excellence, and the highest standards of craftsmanship, is evident in the execution of all our projects to date. Our practice is located in Halifax, Nova Scotia, where proposed projects tend to lack large budgets or extraordinary resources. As a result our team must design and craft our work while pursuing unique and novel ways to add quality or 'value' without the requirement for expensive materials or complicated, time consuming, assemblies.

Peter Braithwaite gründete 2014 die Peter Braithwaite Studio Ltd. aus dem Wunsch heraus, ein Unternehmen zu schaffen, das sowohl Design als auch Bau umfasst. Seit seiner Gründung hat das Unternehmen viele interessante Wohn- und Gewerbeprojekte abgeschlossen und sich im Bereich des Möbel- und Einrichtungsdesigns hervorgetan. Unser Engagement für exzellentes Design und höchste handwerkliche Standards zeigt sich in der Ausführung aller unserer bisherigen Projekte. Unser Büro befindet sich in Halifax, Nova Scotia, wo die vorgeschlagenen Projekte in der Regel nicht über große Budgets oder außergewöhnliche Ressourcen verfügen. Daher muss unser Team bei der Planung und Ausführung unserer Arbeiten einzigartige und neuartige Wege beschreiten, um die Qualität oder den „Wert" zu steigern, ohne dass teure Materialien oder komplizierte, zeitaufwändige Montagen erforderlich sind.

Peter Braithwaite a fondé Peter Braithwaite Studio Ltd. en 2014 dans le but de créer une entreprise englobant à la fois la conception et la construction. Depuis sa création, l'entreprise a réalisé de nombreux projets résidentiels et commerciaux intéressants, et s'est illustrée dans la conception de meubles et d'armoires. Notre dévouement à l'excellence en matière de conception et aux normes les plus élevées de l'artisanat est évident dans l'exécution de tous nos projets à ce jour. Notre pratique est située à Halifax, en Nouvelle-Écosse, où les projets proposés ont tendance à manquer de grands budgets ou de ressources extraordinaires. En conséquence, notre équipe doit concevoir et fabriquer notre travail tout en recherchant des moyens uniques et novateurs d'ajouter de la qualité ou de la « valeur » sans nécessiter de matériaux coûteux ou d'assemblages compliqués et longs.

Peter fundó Peter Braithwaite Studio Ltd. en 2014 por el deseo de crear una empresa que abarcara tanto el diseño como la construcción. Desde su creación, la empresa ha completado numerosos e interesantes proyectos residenciales y comerciales, y ha destacado en el diseño de ebanistería y mobiliario. La excelencia en el diseño y los más altos estándares de artesanía son evidentes en la ejecución de todos los proyectos hasta la fecha. Nuestro despacho se encuentra en Halifax, Nueva Escocia, donde los proyectos propuestos suelen carecer de grandes presupuestos o recursos extraordinarios. Como resultado, nuestro equipo debe diseñar y elaborar nuestro trabajo buscando formas únicas y novedosas de añadir calidad o «valor» sin necesidad de materiales caros o montajes complicados y lentos.

GREAT
GOOD TO GREAT
DEAR EDWARD
HOWARD STERN COMES AGAIN

Generous windows, local materials, and meticulous craftsmanship define Peter Braithwaite Studio's resilient and thoughtful coastal home.

CASA PRIMERIZA

Seamlessly integrated into its cypress-lined hill, this home harmonizes open, light-filled interiors with thoughtful outdoor spaces for a truly immersive experience.

Located on a small clearing within a cypress-filled hill sloping steeply toward the Pacific Ocean in Matanzas, Chile, Casa Primeriza was designed to encompass various moods and environments throughout the house. At the clients' request, it seamlessly integrates into the terrain, allowing occupants to utilize its multiple exterior spaces and make the most of outdoor living.
Anchored firmly atop its solid concrete base, the lighter and airier living spaces span two levels, with the main floor transitioning to the upper level through a double-height space. A cargo netting with an open weave divides this area, inviting children's play while facilitating uninterrupted family life between the two floors. Changes in the wood treatment, both in texture and color, enhance distinct atmospheres between the two floors.

Située sur une petite clairière au sein d'une colline remplie de cyprès descendant abruptement vers l'océan Pacifique à Matanzas, au Chili, Casa Primeriza a été conçue pour englober diverses humeurs et ambiances tout au long de la maison. À la demande des clients, elle s'intègre harmonieusement dans le terrain, permettant aux occupants d'utiliser ses multiples espaces extérieurs et de profiter au maximum de la vie en plein air.
Ancrés fermement au sommet de leur base en béton solide, les espaces de vie plus légers et aérés s'étendent sur deux niveaux, le rez-de-chaussée se transformant en étage supérieur par le biais d'un espace à double hauteur. Un filet de chargement avec une maille ouverte divise cet espace, invitant au jeu des enfants tout en facilitant une vie familiale ininterrompue entre les deux étages. Des changements dans le traitement du bois, tant en texture qu'en couleur, renforcent les atmosphères distinctes entre les deux étages.

Die Casa Primeriza befindet sich auf einer kleinen Lichtung inmitten eines mit Zypressen bewachsenen Hügels, der steil zum Pazifik in Matanzas, Chile, abfällt. Auf Wunsch der Bauherren fügt sich das Haus nahtlos in das Gelände ein und ermöglicht es den Bewohnern, die verschiedenen Außenbereiche zu nutzen und das Leben im Freien optimal zu gestalten.
Auf dem soliden Betonsockel fest verankert, erstrecken sich die leichteren und luftigeren Wohnräume über zwei Ebenen, wobei das Hauptgeschoss durch einen doppelt so hohen Raum in das Obergeschoss übergeht. Ein Cargo-Netz mit offenem Geflecht teilt diesen Bereich und lädt die Kinder zum Spielen ein, während es gleichzeitig ein ungestörtes Familienleben zwischen den beiden Etagen ermöglicht. Veränderungen in der Holzbehandlung, sowohl in der Textur als auch in der Farbe, verstärken die unterschiedlichen Atmosphären zwischen den beiden Etagen.

Situada en un pequeño claro dentro de una colina llena de cipreses con una pronunciada pendiente hacia el Océano Pacífico en Matanzas, Chile, Casa Primeriza fue diseñada para abarcar varios estados de ánimo y ambientes en toda la casa. A petición de los clientes, se integra perfectamente en el terreno, lo que permite a los ocupantes utilizar sus múltiples espacios exteriores y aprovechar al máximo la vida al aire libre.
Anclados firmemente sobre su sólida base de hormigón, los espacios habitables, más ligeros y ventilados, abarcan dos niveles, con la planta principal en transición al nivel superior a través de un espacio de doble altura. Una red de carga con trama abierta divide esta zona, invitando al juego de los niños y facilitando al mismo tiempo la vida familiar ininterrumpida entre las dos plantas. Los cambios en el tratamiento de la madera, tanto en textura como en color, realzan los distintos ambientes entre las dos plantas.

Photos: © Marcos Zegers

Surf
Shacks

STANAĆEV GRANADOS

Nataša Stanaćev, Manu Granados

Stanaćev Granados is a an architectural office founded by Nataša Stanaćev and Manu Granados, Serbian and Spanish architects respectively, with a base in Chile and Spain, and working internationally.
Our practice specializes in bespoke residential projects, characterized by a unique sensitivity toward the domestic life and material tactility. With each new project, we embrace a humble stance and allow our work to surge in a process where we genuinely listen to the clients' needs and meticulously explore the natural and material context of the project. Through innovative approaches and rigorous attention to detail, we strive to create singular and sustainable solutions that seamlessly blend into their surroundings.

Stanaćev Granados ist ein von Nataša Stanaćev und Manu Granados, einem serbischen bzw. spanischen Architekten, gegründetes Architekturbüro mit Sitz in Chile und Spanien, das international tätig ist.
Unser Büro hat sich auf maßgeschneiderte Wohnprojekte spezialisiert, die sich durch eine einzigartige Sensibilität für das häusliche Leben und die Taktilität der Materialien auszeichnen. Bei jedem neuen Projekt nehmen wir eine bescheidene Haltung ein und lassen unsere Arbeit in einem Prozess wachsen, in dem wir den Bedürfnissen der Kunden wirklich zuhören und den natürlichen und materiellen Kontext des Projekts sorgfältig erforschen. Durch innovative Ansätze und rigorose Liebe zum Detail streben wir danach, einzigartige und nachhaltige Lösungen zu schaffen, die sich nahtlos in ihre Umgebung einfügen und außergewöhnliche Alltagserlebnisse ermöglichen.

Stanaćev Granados est un bureau d'architecture fondé par Nataša Stanaćev et Manu Granados, architectes serbes et espagnols respectivement, avec une base au Chili et en Espagne, et travaillant à l'international.
Notre pratique est spécialisée dans les projets résidentiels sur mesure, caractérisés par une sensibilité unique envers la vie domestique et la tactilité des matériaux. Avec chaque nouveau projet, nous adoptons une approche humble et permettons à notre travail de surgir dans un processus où nous écoutons véritablement les besoins des clients et explorons méticuleusement le contexte naturel et matériel du projet. Grâce à des approches innovantes et une attention rigoureuse aux détails, nous nous efforçons de créer des solutions singulières et durables qui s'intègrent harmonieusement à leur environnement.

Stanaćev Granados es un estudio de arquitectura fundado por Nataša Stanaćev y Manu Granados, arquitectos serbio y español respectivamente, con sede en Chile y España, y que trabaja a nivel internacional.
Nuestro estudio se especializa en proyectos residenciales a medida, caracterizados por una sensibilidad única hacia la vida doméstica y la tactilidad de los materiales. Con cada nuevo proyecto, adoptamos una postura humilde y permitimos que nuestro trabajo surja en un proceso en el que escuchamos genuinamente las necesidades de los clientes y exploramos meticulosamente el contexto natural y material del proyecto. Mediante enfoques innovadores y una rigurosa atención al detalle, nos esforzamos por crear soluciones singulares y sostenibles que se integren perfectamente en su entorno.

Layered wood treatments and playful design details highlight Stanaćev Granados' approach to creating engaging, family-friendly living environments.

Valle de Bravo, Mexico

CASA VALLE

A sensitive transformation blending classic charm with Japanese influences, where wood, light, and crafted details create a serene dialogue between architecture and nature.

Casa Valle is a harmonious fusion of renovation and architectural expansion, especially noticeable in the transformation of the old bay, built in the "Chalet" style.
The house features a main extension inspired by the Japanese "engawa" concept, characterised by two horizontal planes that facilitate a seamless connection between the interior and exterior. The raised floor and roof establish a tactile link with nature. Wood was incorporated throughout the project, from the structure to the interior finishes and furniture design, fostering an atmosphere of warmth, serenity and a perfect balance between the modern and the classic. At Casa Valle, every detail was designed. We believe in the importance of craftsmanship, detail and landscape integration.

Casa Valle est une fusion harmonieuse de rénovation et d'agrandissement architectural, particulièrement perceptible dans la transformation de l'ancienne baie, construite dans le style « Chalet ».
La maison présente une extension principale inspirée du concept japonais « engawa », caractérisée par deux plans horizontaux facilitant une connexion sans faille entre l'intérieur et l'extérieur. Le sol surélevé et le toit établissent un lien tactile avec la nature. Le bois a été incorporé dans tout le projet, de la structure aux finitions intérieures et au design des meubles, favorisant une atmosphère de chaleur, de sérénité et un équilibre parfait entre le moderne et le classique. À Casa Valle, chaque détail a été conçu. Nous croyons en l'importance de l'artisanat, du détail et de l'intégration paysagère.

Casa Valle ist eine harmonische Verschmelzung von Renovierung und architektonischer Erweiterung, die sich besonders in der Umgestaltung des alten Erkers im Chalet-Stil zeigt.
Das Haus verfügt über einen Hauptanbau, der vom japanischen „engawa"-Konzept inspiriert ist und sich durch zwei horizontale Ebenen auszeichnet, die eine nahtlose Verbindung zwischen Innen und Außen ermöglichen. Der Doppelboden und das Dach stellen eine taktile Verbindung zur Natur her. Holz wurde im gesamten Projekt verwendet, von der Struktur bis hin zu den Innenausstattungen und dem Möbeldesign, wodurch eine Atmosphäre der Wärme, der Gelassenheit und des perfekten Gleichgewichts zwischen Moderne und Klassik geschaffen wurde. Bei Casa Valle wurde jedes Detail geplant. Wir glauben an die Bedeutung von Handwerkskunst, Details und die Integration der Landschaft.

Casa Valle es una fusión armoniosa de renovación y expansión arquitectónica, especialmente notoria en la transformación de la antigua crujía, construida en el estilo «Chalet».
La casa presenta una extensión principal inspirada en el concepto japonés «engawa», caracterizada por dos planos horizontales que facilitan una conexión fluida entre el interior y el exterior. El suelo elevado y el techo establecen un vínculo táctil con la naturaleza. La madera se incorporó en todo el proyecto, desde la estructura hasta los acabados interiores y el diseño del mobiliario, fomentando una atmósfera de calidez, serenidad y un equilibrio perfecto entre lo moderno y lo clásico. En la Casa Valle, cada detalle fue diseñado. Creemos en la importancia de la artesanía, el detalle y la integración del paisaje.

Photos: © Camila Cossio

STUDIO HEYA

Nathalie Franquebalme

Studio Heya is an architecture and design studio founded by Nathalie Franquebalme in 2020 in Tokyo, and based in Mexico City since 2023. Studio Heya questions, explores and designs regardless of being in different social, political and geographical contexts. It works between architecture, art and research, proposing schemes of collective creation. His work arises from observation and a multidisciplinary plastic process that helps the understanding of the site or object and gives input and guidance to the architecture and design. Studio Heya works on projects of different scales, from a Master plan, an architectural project, to furniture and object design. Nathalie has collaborated with Alberto Kalach, Nikken Sekkei and Kengo Kuma & Associates.

Studio Heya ist ein Architektur- und Designstudio, das 2020 von Nathalie Franquebalme in Tokio gegründet wurde und seit 2023 in Mexiko-Stadt ansässig ist. Das Studio Heya hinterfragt, erforscht und entwirft unabhängig von verschiedenen sozialen, politischen und geografischen Kontexten. Es arbeitet an der Schnittstelle zwischen Architektur, Kunst und Forschung und schlägt Schemata kollektiven Schaffens vor. Seine Arbeit entsteht aus der Beobachtung und einem multidisziplinären plastischen Prozess, der zum Verständnis des Ortes oder Objekts beiträgt und der Architektur und dem Design Input und Anleitung gibt. Das Studio Heya arbeitet an Projekten unterschiedlicher Größenordnung, von einem Masterplan über ein Architekturprojekt bis hin zu Möbel- und Objektdesign. Nathalie hat mit Alberto Kalach, Nikken Sekkei und Kengo Kuma & Associates zusammengearbeitet.

Studio Heya est un studio d'architecture et de design fondé par Nathalie Franquebalme en 2020 à Tokyo, et basé à Mexico depuis 2023. Studio Heya questionne, explore et conçoit indépendamment des contextes sociaux, politiques et géographiques différents. Il travaille entre l'architecture, l'art et la recherche, proposant des schémas de création collective. Son travail découle de l'observation et d'un processus plastique multidisciplinaire qui aide à la compréhension du site ou de l'objet et donne des informations et des orientations à l'architecture et au design. Studio Heya travaille sur des projets de différentes échelles, d'un plan directeur à un projet architectural, en passant par le design de meubles et d'objets. Nathalie a collaboré avec Alberto Kalach, Nikken Sekkei et Kengo Kuma & Associates.

Studio Heya es un taller de arquitectura y diseño fundado por Nathalie Franquebalme en 2020 en la ciudad de Tokio, y con sede en Ciudad de México desde 2023. Studio Heya cuestiona, explora y diseña sin importar encontrarse en diferentes contextos sociales, políticos y geográficos. Trabaja entre la arquitectura, el arte y la investigación planteando esquemas de creación colectiva. Su trabajo surge de la observación y de un proceso multidisciplinario plástico que ayuda al entendimiento del sitio u objeto y dan entrada y pauta a la arquitectura y al diseño. Studio Heya trabaja en proyectos de diferentes escalas, desde un Máster plan, un proyecto arquitectónico, hasta el diseño de mobiliario y de objetos. Nathalie ha colaborado con Alberto Kalach, Nikken Sekkei y Kengo Kuma & Associates.

Studio Heya reimagines tradition through meticulous craftsmanship, integrating architecture with its environment to craft spaces of subtle beauty and timeless connection.

DOM LAS

Inspired by Kashubia's vernacular style, this Polish retreat combines local materials and meticulous craftsmanship, blending family legacy with harmonious design.

DOM LAS ("Forest House" in Polish) is a project born from a specific situation. 25 years ago, the client bought an empty field near his hometown, with the vision to create something for the future. Through care and attention, the 7 hectares have been transformed into an attractive and varied landscape, reflecting the native flora of the region. The buildings are a result of a conversation between the vernacular style of Poland's Kashubia region, the traditional materials of the area and the natural environment. Although the brief was minimal, the building needed to serve two different but complimentary functions: to enable the continued care of the land, but also offer occasional shelter for the client and his family. The result is two buildings which have a relationship to each other, but also to the landscape in which they are placed. This is emphasized through the materials used and details incorporated, the craftsmanship of local skilled workers, and the celebration of family heirlooms.

DOM LAS (« Maison de la Forêt » en polonais) est un projet né d'une situation spécifique. Il y a 25 ans, le client a acheté un champ vide près de sa ville natale, avec la vision de créer quelque chose pour l'avenir. Grâce au soin et à l'attention, les 7 hectares se sont transformés en un paysage attrayant et varié reflétant la flore native de la région. Les bâtiments sont le résultat d'une conversation entre le style vernaculaire de la région de Cachoubie en Pologne et les matériaux traditionnels. Bien que les instructions fussent minimales, le bâtiment devait remplir deux fonctions différentes mais complémentaires : permettre l'entretien continu du terrain, mais aussi offrir un abri occasionnel au client et à sa famille. Le résultat sont deux bâtiments qui ont une relation entre eux, mais aussi avec le paysage dans lequel ils sont situés. Cela est souligné à travers les matériaux utilisés et les détails incorporés, l'artisanat de travailleurs locaux spécialisés et la célébration des reliques familiales.

DOM LAS („Waldhaus" auf Polnisch) ist ein Projekt, das vor 25 Jahren entstand. Der Bauherr kaufte ein Feld in der Nähe seiner Heimatstadt mit der Vision, etwas für die Zukunft zu schaffen. Durch Sorgfalt und Aufmerksamkeit wurden die 7 Hektar in eine attraktive und vielfältige Landschaft verwandelt, die die einheimische Flora der Region widerspiegelt. Die Gebäude sind das Ergebnis eines Dialogs zwischen dem volkstümlichen Stil der Region Kaschubei in Polen und den traditionellen Materialien. Obwohl die Anweisungen minimal waren, musste das Gebäude zwei verschiedene, aber ergänzende Funktionen erfüllen: die kontinuierliche Pflege des Geländes ermöglichen, aber auch gelegentlich Schutz für den Kunden und seine Familie bieten. Das Ergebnis sind zwei Gebäude, die sowohl miteinander als auch mit der Landschaft, in der sie sich befinden, in Beziehung stehen. Dies wird durch die verwendeten Materialien und die eingebauten Details, das Handwerk lokaler spezialisierter Arbeiter und die Feier von Familienerbstücken betont.

DOM LAS («Casa del Bosque» en polaco) es un proyecto nacido de una situación específica. Hace 25 años, el cliente compró un campo vacío cerca de su ciudad natal, con la visión de crear algo para el futuro. A través del cuidado y la atención, las 7 ha. se han transformado en un paisaje atractivo y variado que refleja la flora nativa de la región. Los edificios son el resultado de una conversación entre el estilo vernáculo de la región de Kashubia de Polonia y los materiales tradicionales. Aunque las instrucciones fueron mínimas, el edificio necesitaba cumplir dos funciones diferentes pero complementarias: permitir el cuidado continuo del terreno, pero también ofrecer refugio ocasional para el cliente y su familia. El resultado son dos edificios que tienen una relación entre sí, pero también con el paisaje en el que están ubicados. Esto se enfatiza a través de los materiales utilizados y los detalles incorporados, la artesanía de trabajadores locales especializados y la celebración de reliquias familiares.

Photos: © Martyna Rudnicka

PORCELANA EUROPEJSKA

HISTORIA SZTUKI 1
HISTORIA SZTUKI 2
HISTORIA SZTUKI 3
HISTORIA SZTUKI 4

STUDIO ONU

Kuba Tomaszczyk

Studio Onu's philosophy is to create designs with the potential to carry a narrative to the future. It begins every design by learning about the client; their personality, background, passions, and dreams – this all has an impact, informing each proposal. The natural environment and regionally-sourced treasures of a project's location influence its design, and attention to these details forms a defining quality of Studio Onu's work. Architecture goes far beyond the physical walls. Founded in 2020 by UK-trained architect Kuba Tomaszczyk, Studio Onu is an award-winning Basel-based practice, working internationally. Its current focus is on small scale rural projects in Poland, Switzerland and Denmark.

Die Philosophie von Studio Onu ist es, Designs mit dem Potenzial zu schaffen, eine Erzählung in die Zukunft zu transportieren. Es beginnt jedes Design, indem es den Kunden kennenlernt: ihre Persönlichkeit, Hintergründe, Leidenschaften und Träume, die alle eine Auswirkung haben und jeden Vorschlag informieren. Die natürliche Umgebung und die regionalen Schätze des Standorts eines Projekts beeinflussen sein Design, und die Aufmerksamkeit für diese Details bildet eine bestimmende Qualität der Arbeit von Studio Onu. Architektur geht weit über physische Wände hinaus. 2020 von dem in Großbritannien ausgebildeten Architekten Kuba Tomaszczyk gegründet, ist Studio Onu ein preisgekröntes Büro mit Sitz in Basel, das international arbeitet. Sein aktueller Fokus liegt auf ländlichen Kleinskalaprojekten in Polen, der Schweiz und Dänemark.

La philosophie de Studio Onu est de créer des designs avec le potentiel de transmettre une narration vers l'avenir. Il commence chaque conception en apprenant sur le client ; sa personnalité, son parcours, ses passions et ses rêves, tout cela ayant un impact et influençant chaque proposition. L'environnement naturel et les trésors d'origine régionale de l'emplacement d'un projet influent sur sa conception, et l'attention portée à ces détails forme une qualité déterminante du travail de Studio Onu. L'architecture va bien au-delà des murs physiques. Fondé en 2020 par l'architecte formé au Royaume-Uni Kuba Tomaszczyk, Studio Onu est un cabinet basé à Bâle, primé et travaillant à l'international. Son focus actuel est sur des projets ruraux de petite échelle en Pologne, en Suisse et au Danemark.

La filosofía de Studio Onu es crear diseños con el potencial de transmitir una narrativa hacia el futuro. Comienza cada diseño aprendiendo sobre el cliente; su personalidad, antecedentes, pasiones y sueños, todo esto tiene un impacto e informa cada propuesta. El entorno natural y los tesoros de origen regional de la ubicación de un proyecto influyen en su diseño, y la atención a estos detalles forma una cualidad definitoria del trabajo de Studio Onu. La arquitectura va mucho más allá de las paredes físicas. Fundada en 2020 por el arquitecto entrenado en el Reino Unido Kuba Tomaszczyk, Studio Onu es un despacho con sede en Basilea, galardonado y que trabaja internacionalmente. Su enfoque actual se centra en proyectos rurales de pequeña escala en Polonia, Suiza y Dinamarca.

The interplay of traditional techniques and family heirlooms exemplifies Studio Onu's commitment to storytelling through architecture.

APARTMENT XVIII

A tranquil space inspired by history, Apartment XVIII harmonizes natural light, curved forms, and soft finishes for a serene Parisian retreat.

This flat overlooking the Luxembourg Gardens is located in a former 18th century mansion that was remodelled in the years after the French Revolution. Since so little of the original features remained and major structural reinforcements had to be made, it was decided to demolish the existing and create a project based on the feelings inspired by the place. The home is located in one of the oldest areas of Paris and surrounded by a fantastic landscape of private buildings, churches, convents and squares, so architect Alireza Razavi imagined a monastic space. Natural light, which enters from three different directions, has been the main raw material. The quality of the building is expressed in the interior with generous load-bearing walls and columns, further emphasising its materiality with the application of a plaster stucco that rubs against the light. The selection of soft finishes and the abundant use of curved shapes to avoid harsh shadows has created a tranquil space, where sound, light and vision form part of a coherent whole.

Cet appartement, qui donne sur les jardins du Luxembourg, est situé dans un ancien hôtel particulier du XVIIIe siècle, remodelé dans les années qui ont suivi la Révolution française. Comme il ne restait que très peu d'éléments d'origine et que d'importants renforcements structurels devaient être effectués, il a été décidé de démolir l'existant et de créer un projet basé sur les sentiments inspirés par le lieu. La maison est située dans l'un des plus anciens quartiers de Paris et entourée d'un paysage fantastique de bâtiments privés, d'églises, de couvents et de places. L'architecte Alireza Razavi a donc imaginé un espace monastique. La lumière naturelle, qui entre par trois directions différentes, a été la principale matière première. La qualité du bâtiment s'exprime à l'intérieur par des murs porteurs et des colonnes généreuses, soulignant encore sa matérialité par l'application d'un stuc plâtreux qui se frotte à la lumière. La sélection de finitions douces et l'utilisation abondante de formes courbes pour éviter les ombres dures ont créé un espace tranquille, où le son, la lumière et la vision font partie d'un tout cohérent.

Diese Wohnung mit Blick auf die Luxemburger Gärten befindet sich in einem ehemaligen Herrenhaus aus dem 18. Jahrhundert, das in den Jahren nach der Französischen Revolution umgebaut wurde. Da so wenig von der ursprünglichen Bausubstanz erhalten geblieben war und erhebliche strukturelle Verstärkungen vorgenommen werden mussten, wurde beschlossen, das bestehende Gebäude abzureißen und ein Projekt zu schaffen, das auf den von diesem Ort inspirierten Gefühlen basiert. Das Haus befindet sich in einem der ältesten Viertel von Paris und ist von einer fantastischen Landschaft mit privaten Gebäuden, Kirchen, Klöstern und Plätzen umgeben, so dass der Architekt Alireza Razavi sich einen klösterlichen Raum vorgestellt hat. Natürliches Licht, das aus drei verschiedenen Richtungen einfällt, war das wichtigste Ausgangsmaterial. Die Qualität des Gebäudes kommt im Inneren mit großzügigen tragenden Wänden und Säulen zum Ausdruck, wobei die Materialität des Gebäudes durch die Verwendung eines Gipsstucks, der sich am Licht reibt, noch betont wird. Durch die Auswahl weicher Oberflächen und die reichliche Verwendung geschwungener Formen zur Vermeidung harter Schatten wurde ein ruhiger Raum geschaffen, in dem Klang, Licht und Sicht ein kohärentes Ganzes bilden.

Este apartamento con vistas a los jardines de Luxemburgo, se encuentra en una antigua mansión del siglo XVIII remodelada en los años posteriores a la revolución francesa. Puesto que quedaba tan poco de las características originales y había que hacer importantes refuerzos estructurales, se optó por demoler lo existente y crear un proyecto a partir de los sentimientos que inspiraba el lugar. La vivienda está situada en una de las zonas más antiguas de París y rodeada de un fantástico paisaje de edificios privados, iglesias, conventos y plazas, por ello el arquitecto Alireza Razavi imaginó un espacio monástico. La luz natural que entra desde tres direcciones diferentes, ha sido la principal materia prima. La calidad del edificio se expresa en el interior con generosos muros de carga y columnas, resaltando además su materialidad con la aplicación de un estuco de yeso que roza con la luz. La selección de acabados suaves y el uso abundante de las formas curvas para evitar las sombras duras, ha creado un espacio tranquilo, donde el sonido, la luz y la visión forman parte de un todo coherente.

Photos: © Vincent Leroux

ROMAN

STUDIO RAZAVI ARCHITECTURE

Alireza Razavi

Alireza Razavi (1970) is a registered architect in France, a licensed professional in the United States, and a Chartered Architect in the UK. He holds a Master's Degree from Columbia University in New York and a Master's Degree from the Ecole Nationale des Arts Décoratifs in Paris. Selected as an AD100 Best Designer for 4 consecutive years, his designs cover a wide spectrum or architectural services from interiors to master planning for clients in both the public and private sectors. Operating as one firm with three offices (Paris, New York and London) the studio's portfolio of works spans from Europe to the Americas and includes residential, corporate, hospitality, civic, transportation, and mixed-use projects.

Alireza Razavi (1970) ist in Frankreich und im Vereinigten Königreich als Architekt eingetragen und in den Vereinigten Staaten als Fachmann zugelassen. Er hat einen Master-Abschluss von der Columbia University in New York und einen weiteren von der Ecole Nationale des Arts Décoratifs in Paris. Seine Arbeit, die in vier aufeinander folgenden Jahren als AD100 Best Designer ausgezeichnet wurde, umfasst ein breites Spektrum an architektonischen Dienstleistungen, von Innenräumen bis hin zur Masterplanung. Das Büro verfügt über drei Niederlassungen (Paris, New York und London), und sein Portfolio erstreckt sich von Europa bis nach Amerika mit Projekten in den Bereichen Wohnen, Unternehmen, Gastgewerbe, öffentliche Einrichtungen, Verkehr und Mischnutzung.

Alireza Razavi (1970) est un architecte agréé en France et au Royaume-Uni, et un professionnel agréé aux États-Unis. Il est titulaire d'une maîtrise de l'université Columbia de New York et d'une autre de l'École nationale des arts décoratifs de Paris. Sélectionné comme meilleur designer de l'AD100 pendant quatre années consécutives, son travail couvre un large éventail de services architecturaux, de l'intérieur à la planification générale. Le studio fonctionne comme une entreprise avec trois bureaux (Paris, New York et Londres) et son portefeuille de travaux s'étend de l'Europe à l'Amérique avec des projets résidentiels, d'entreprise, d'hospitalité, civiques, de transport et à usage mixte.

Alireza Razavi (1970) es un arquitecto colegiado en Francia, y el Reino Unido, y profesional autorizado en Estados Unidos. Cuenta con un máster de la Universidad de Columbia en Nueva York, y otro de la Escuela Nacional de Artes Decorativas de París. Seleccionado como mejor diseñador del AD100 durante 4 años consecutivos, sus trabajos abarcan un amplio espectro de servicios arquitectónicos que van desde los interiores hasta la planificación maestra. El estudio opera como una empresa con tres oficinas (París, Nueva York y Londres) y su cartera de trabajos se extiende desde Europa hasta América con proyectos residenciales, corporativos, hospitalarios, cívicos, de transporte y de uso mixto.

Generous walls, curved shapes, and subtle textures reflect Alireza Razavi's vision of a calm, light-filled haven within a historic Parisian setting.

L'ART CISTERCIEN

CHANEL

KARRI LOAM

A tranquil retreat blending rammed earth, natural timber, and minimalist design, Karri Loam invites stillness amidst the ancient Karri Forest.

Conceived as a retreat or short-term rental house, Karri Loam is located in a residential area overlooking the ancient Karri Forest on the Margaret River. The building has two levels that define the design concept through two different experiences. On the ground floor the occupant is immersed in the solidity of the rammed earth walls, but is liberated when, via a wooden staircase, he or she enters the light space of the first floor, facing the treetops. All excess is deliberately omitted. Clean surfaces, neutral tones and essential, comfortable furnishings reduce visual noise and draw the eye inwards. The materials are inspired by the early country houses built in the 80's with local and accessible materials. The project uses a local mix of lime and eucalyptus sediment for the steady earth walls. The paints are natural lime and the timbers are Australian, many of which were naturally fallen. To enhance the tactile qualities of the materials they worked with local craftsmen who shaped the rough sawn eucalyptus boards, and the highly skilled finish of the micro-cement surfaces.

Conçu comme une retraite ou une maison de location à court terme, Karri Loam est situé dans une zone résidentielle surplombant l'ancienne forêt de Karri sur la Margaret River. Le bâtiment comporte deux niveaux qui définissent le concept de design à travers deux expériences différentes. Au rez-de-chaussée, l'occupant est immergé dans la solidité des murs en terre battue, mais il est libéré lorsque, par un escalier en bois, il pénètre dans l'espace lumineux du premier étage, face à la cime des arbres. Tout excès est délibérément omis. Des surfaces propres, des tons neutres et un mobilier essentiel et confortable réduisent le bruit visuel et attirent le regard vers l'intérieur. Les matériaux sont inspirés des premières maisons de campagne construites dans les années 80 avec des matériaux locaux et accessibles. Le projet utilise un mélange local de chaux et de sédiment d'eucalyptus pour les murs en terre stabilisée. Les peintures sont à la chaux naturelle et les bois sont australiens, dont beaucoup sont tombés naturellement. Pour améliorer les qualités tactiles des matériaux, ils ont travaillé avec des artisans locaux qui ont façonné les planches d'eucalyptus brutes de sciage, et la finition hautement qualifiée des surfaces en microciment.

Karri Loam wurde als Rückzugsort oder als Haus für Kurzzeitmieten konzipiert und befindet sich in einem Wohngebiet mit Blick auf den alten Karri Forest am Margaret River. Das Gebäude besteht aus zwei Ebenen, die das Designkonzept durch zwei unterschiedliche Erfahrungen definieren. Im Erdgeschoss ist der Bewohner in die Solidität der Stampflehmwände eingetaucht, wird aber befreit, wenn er über eine Holztreppe in den hellen Raum des ersten Stocks mit Blick auf die Baumkronen gelangt. Auf alles Überflüssige wird bewusst verzichtet. Klare Oberflächen, neutrale Töne und wesentliche, bequeme Einrichtungsgegenstände reduzieren den visuellen Lärm und lenken den Blick nach innen. Die Materialien sind von den frühen Landhäusern inspiriert, die in den 80er Jahren mit lokalen und zugänglichen Materialien gebaut wurden. Das Projekt verwendet eine lokale Mischung aus Kalk und Eukalyptussediment für die festen Lehmwände. Die Farben sind aus natürlichem Kalk und die Hölzer aus Australien, von denen viele natürlich gefallen sind. Um die taktilen Qualitäten der Materialien hervorzuheben, arbeiteten sie mit lokalen Handwerkern zusammen, die die sägerauen Eukalyptusbretter und die hochqualifizierte Oberfläche des Mikrozements formten.

Concebida como una casa para retiros o de alquiler de corta duración, Karri Loam se encuentra en un pueblo mirando hacia el antiguo bosque de Karri, en el río Margaret. La construcción tiene dos niveles que definen el concepto de diseño a través de dos experiencias diferentes. En la planta baja el ocupante está inmerso en la solidez de los muros de tierra apisonada, pero se libera cuando a través de una escalera de madera, se adentra en el espacio ligero orientado hacia las copas de los árboles en la segunda planta. Todo exceso está omitido a propósito. Superficies limpias, tonos neutros y mobiliario esencial y confortable reducen el ruido visual y llevan la mirada hacia el interior. Los materiales de la obra se inspiran en las casas de campo construidas por sus habitantes con materiales de la zona. El proyecto utiliza una mezcla local de cal y sedimento de eucaliptus para los muros de tierra estabilizada. Las pinturas son de cal natural y las maderas australianas y principalmente caídas de forma natural. Para realzar las cualidades táctiles de los materiales se trabajó con artesanos locales que dieron forma a las tablas de eucaliptus aserradas en bruto, y al acabado altamente cualificado de las superficies de microcemento.

STUDIO STOOKS

Ash Stucken
Collaborator: Miranda Geiger

Studio Stooks focuses on connecting nature and architecture through rigorous design that links place and person. Director, Ash Stucken's buildings are intended to be a reflection of their place, time and people and are made with the intention of ageing gracefully. His overall aim is to achieve timelessness in a fast-moving industry and world. Ash Stucken and Miranda Geiger's collaborative work on Karri Loam seeks to celebrate the passage of time and encourage a sense of being present. Tactility is a strong theme that is explored through natural materials and craftsmanship, experimenting with contrasting finishes, from raw and rough, to minimalist and refined.

Das Studio Stooks konzentriert sich auf die Verbindung von Natur und Architektur durch strenges Design, das Ort und Mensch miteinander verbindet. Die Gebäude des Direktors Ash Stucken sollen den Ort, die Zeit und die Menschen widerspiegeln und mit der Absicht gebaut werden, anmutig zu altern. Sein übergeordnetes Ziel ist es, in einer schnelllebigen Industrie und Welt Zeitlosigkeit zu erreichen. Ash Stucken und Miranda Geiger wollen mit ihrer gemeinsamen Arbeit an Karri Loam das Vergehen der Zeit feiern und ein Gefühl der Gegenwärtigkeit fördern. Taktilität ist ein starkes Thema, das durch natürliche Materialien und Handwerkskunst erforscht wird, wobei mit kontrastreichen Oberflächen experimentiert wird, von roh und rau bis hin zu minimalistisch und raffiniert.

Le Studio Stooks s'attache à relier la nature et l'architecture par une conception rigoureuse qui établit un lien entre le lieu et la personne. Les bâtiments du directeur, Ash Stucken, se veulent le reflet de leur lieu, de leur époque et de leurs habitants et sont conçus dans l'intention de vieillir avec élégance. Son objectif global est d'atteindre l'intemporalité dans un secteur et un monde en évolution rapide. Le travail de collaboration d'Ash Stucken et Miranda Geiger sur Karri Loam cherche à célébrer le passage du temps et à encourager le sentiment d'être présent. La tactilité est un thème fort qui est exploré à travers les matériaux naturels et l'artisanat, en expérimentant des finitions contrastées, allant du brut et de la rugosité au minimaliste et au raffiné.

Studio Stooks se centra en conectar la naturaleza y la arquitectura a través de un diseño riguroso que vincula lugar y persona. Los edificios de su director, Ash Stucken, pretenden ser un reflejo de su lugar, su tiempo y su gente, y están hechos con la intención de envejecer con gracia. Su objetivo general es lograr la atemporalidad en un sector y un mundo que evoluciona con rapidez. El trabajo conjunto de Ash Stucken y Miranda Geiger en Karri Loam pretende celebrar el paso del tiempo y fomentar la sensación de estar presente. El tacto es un tema importante que se explora a través de materiales naturales y artesanía, experimentando con acabados contrastados, desde crudos y ásperos hasta minimalistas y refinados.

Locally sourced materials and handcrafted finishes reflect Studio Stooks' philosophy of connecting architecture to place, fostering timelessness and presence.

Guerrero, Mexico

CASA DEL ACANTILADO

Drawing from the cliffs of Zihuatanejo, this home seamlessly integrates vernacular techniques and contemporary comfort in harmony with its natural surroundings.

Perched on cliffs battered by the force of the sea, this house is located in the bay of Zihuatanejo, on the Pacific coast. Its position is that of a lighthouse that warns fishermen and provides light. Its spirit is that of the rock from which it emerges, mimicking the context and putting into practice the craft techniques and vernacular architecture of the place. In this project the topography is a determining factor in the spatial layout. The house is entered directly from the upper floor, without an access door. A palapa of stone, wood and palm leaves is made by local labour, welcoming and housing the social area exposed to the cliffs. Its shape takes advantage of natural light and cross ventilation to reduce energy consumption. The staircase leading to the private area is framed by uncovered concrete walls and terminates in a pool contained by walls that frame the infinity continuity with the Pacific. The foyer links to the bedrooms, each with private terraces that open onto spaces for contemplation of the incredible landscape.

Perchée sur des falaises battues par la force de la mer, cette maison est située dans la baie de Zihuatanejo, sur la côte Pacifique. Sa position est celle d'un phare qui avertit les pêcheurs et fournit de la lumière. Son esprit est celui de la roche d'où il émerge, imitant le contexte et mettant en pratique les techniques artisanales et l'architecture vernaculaire du lieu. Dans ce projet, la topographie est un facteur déterminant dans l'organisation spatiale. On entre directement dans la maison par l'étage supérieur, sans porte d'accès. Une palapa de pierre, de bois et de feuilles de palmier est fabriquée par la main-d'œuvre locale, accueillant et abritant l'espace social exposé aux falaises. Sa forme tire parti de la lumière naturelle et de la ventilation croisée pour réduire la consommation d'énergie. L'escalier menant à la zone privée est encadré par des murs en béton non couverts et se termine par une piscine contenue par des murs qui encadrent la continuité à l'infini avec le Pacifique. Le foyer relie les chambres, chacune avec des terrasses privées qui s'ouvrent sur des espaces de contemplation de l'incroyable paysage.

Dieses Haus liegt in der Bucht von Zihuatanejo an der Pazifikküste auf einer Klippe, die von der Kraft des Meeres umspült wird. Seine Position ist die eines Leuchtturms, der die Fischer warnt und Licht spendet. Der Geist des Felsens, aus dem es entstanden ist, wird durch die Nachahmung des Kontextes und die Umsetzung der handwerklichen Techniken und der volkstümlichen Architektur des Ortes geprägt. Bei diesem Projekt ist die Topographie ein entscheidender Faktor für die räumliche Organisation. Das Haus wird direkt vom Obergeschoss aus betreten, ohne eine Zugangstür. Ein Palapa aus Stein, Holz und Palmblättern wurde von einheimischen Arbeitern errichtet und beherbergt den sozialen Bereich, der den Klippen ausgesetzt ist. Seine Form nutzt das natürliche Licht und die Querlüftung, um den Energieverbrauch zu senken. Die Treppe, die zum privaten Bereich führt, wird von unverkleideten Betonwänden eingerahmt und endet in einem Pool, der von Mauern umgeben ist, die die unendliche Kontinuität mit dem Pazifik einrahmen. Vom Foyer aus gelangt man zu den Schlafzimmern, die alle über private Terrassen verfügen, von denen aus man die unglaubliche Landschaft betrachten kann.

Postrada sobre acantilados golpeados por la fuerza del mar, se encuentra esta casa, en la bahía de Zihuatanejo, costa del Pacífico. Su posición es la de un faro que avisa a los pescadores y proporciona luz. Su espíritu es el de la roca de la que emerge mimetizándose con el contexto y poniendo en práctica las técnicas artesanales y la arquitectura vernácula del sitio. En este proyecto la topografía es un factor determinante para la organización espacial. A la casa se entra directamente desde la planta alta y no hay puerta de acceso. Una palapa da la bienvenida y alberga el área social expuesta a los acantilados. La palapa de piedra, madera y hojas de palma, está hecha por mano de obra local. Su forma aprovecha la luz natural y una ventilación cruzada que reduce el consumo de energía. La escalera de acceso a la zona privada está enmarcada por muros de hormigón descubiertos y terminan en una piscina contenida por muros de que enmarcan la continuidad infinita con el Pacífico. El vestíbulo enlaza con las habitaciones, cada una con terrazas privadas que se abren a espacios de contemplación hacia el increíble paisaje.

Photos: © Rafael Gamo

ZOZAYA ARQUITECTOS

Daniel Zozaya, Enrique Zozaya

Father and son make up this architectural studio linked to the Pacific coast. Enrique Zozaya studied at La Salle University. He worked as a project developer for Ricardo Legorreta and Ramírez Vázquez, which influenced the architecture he developed in the following years in Zihuatanejo, Mexico, where he founded the firm in 1986. His contact with life in the tropics on the coast of Guerrero has allowed him to create his own style, influenced by his daily observation of the climate and nature. Daniel Zozaya, for his part, studied architecture at the Universidad Iberoamericana and his incorporation into the firm in 2015 has involved a leap towards new technologies. He is an expert in creating idyllic private homes that blend the local and the global.

Vater und Sohn bilden dieses Architekturbüro an der Pazifikküste. Enrique Zozaya studierte an der Universität La Salle. Er arbeitete als Projektentwickler für Ricardo Legorreta und Ramírez Vázquez, was die Architektur beeinflusste, die er in den folgenden Jahren in Zihuatanejo, Mexiko, entwickelte, wo er 1986 das Büro gründete. Sein Kontakt mit dem Leben in den Tropen an der Küste von Guerrero hat es ihm ermöglicht, seinen eigenen Stil zu kreieren, der von seinen täglichen Beobachtungen des Klimas und der Natur beeinflusst ist. Daniel Zozaya seinerseits hat an der Universidad Iberoamericana Architektur studiert. Seine Aufnahme in das Büro im Jahr 2015 bedeutete einen Sprung in Richtung neuer Technologien. Er ist Experte für die Gestaltung idyllischer Privathäuser, die das Lokale mit dem Globalen verbinden.

Père et fils composent ce studio d'architecture lié à la côte Pacifique. Enrique Zozaya a étudié à l'université La Salle. Il a travaillé comme développeur de projets pour Ricardo Legorreta et Ramírez Vázquez, ce qui a influencé l'architecture qu'il a développée dans les années suivantes à Zihuatanejo, au Mexique, où il a fondé le cabinet en 1986. Son contact avec la vie sous les tropiques, sur la côte de Guerrero, lui a permis de créer son propre style, influencé par son observation quotidienne du climat et de la nature. Daniel Zozaya, quant à lui, a étudié l'architecture à l'Universidad Iberoamericana et son incorporation au cabinet en 2015 a signifié un saut vers les nouvelles technologies. Il est expert dans la création de résidences privées idylliques qui mêlent le local et le global.

Padre hijo, conforman este estudio de arquitectura ligado a la costa del Pacífico. Enrique Zozaya estudió en la Universidad La Salle. Trabajó como promotor de proyectos para Ricardo Legorreta y Ramírez Vázquez, lo que influyó en la arquitectura que desarrolló en los años siguientes en Zihuatanejo donde fundó el despacho en 1986. Su contacto con la vida del trópico en la costa guerrerense, le ha permitido crear un estilo propio muy influido por la observación cotidiana del clima y la naturaleza. Daniel Zozaya, por su parte, estudió Arquitectura en la Universidad Iberoamericana y su incorporación al despacho en 2015 ha implicado el salto hacia las nuevas tecnologías. Es un experto en la creación de casas privadas idílicas que mezclan lo local y lo global.

Crafted from local materials, the house combines tradition and modernity, illustrating Zozaya Arquitectos' approach to climate-responsive coastal living.

P. 8

AKB ARCHITECTS
Robert Kastelic, Kelly Buffey

www.akb.ca

P. 20

ALTAMAREA ARQUITECTURA
Altamarea Team

www.alta-marea.cl

P. 30

BOSC ARCHITECTES
Jean Bosc, Arthur Bosc

www.bosc-architectes.com

P. 44

BREWIN DESIGN OFFICE
Robert Cheng

www.brewindesignoffice.com

P. 54

CARME PARDO ARQUITECTURA INTERIOR
Carme Pardo

www.carmepardo.es

P. 64

CLO STUDIOS
Chloe Tozer

www.clostudios.com.au

P. 76

CO-LAB DESIGN OFFICE
Joana Gomes, Joshua Beck

www.co-labdesignoffice.com

P. 88

DA BUREAU
Boris Lvovsky, Anna Lvovskaya, Fedor Goreglyad, Maria Romanova

www.da-bureau.com

P. 98

© Nathalie Joly d'Aussy

D'AUSSY INTERIORS
Clara Joly d'Aussy

www.daussyinteriors.com

P. 106

ERLING BERG
Erling Berg

www.erlingberg.com

P. 114

FAMM ARQUITECTURA
Felipe Apestegui, Mariano Mesalles

www.fammarq.com

P. 124

FAR STUDIO
Brittany Hakimfar, Benjamin Hakimfar

www.farstudio.com

P. 138

GOLANY ARCHITECTS
Yaron Golany, Galit Golany

www.golanyarchitects.com

P. 150

GO INTERIORS
Nicole Gottschall

www.go-interiors.ch

P. 160

IDEE ARCHITECTS
Trần Ngọc Linh, Nguyen Huy Hai

www.idee.vn

P. 170

I IN
Yohei Terui, Hiromu Yuyama

www.i-in.jp

P. 180

JESSICA BATAILLE - THE LIFESTYLE COMPANY
Jessica Bataille

www.jessicabataille.com

P. 192

LSD ARCHITECTS
Rodolfo Tinocco, Luis Mauricio Solís

www.lsd.cr

P. 202

MARLENE ULDSCHMIDT STUDIO
Marlene Uldschmidt

www.marleneuldschmidt.com

P. 212

NC DESIGN & ARCHITECTURE
Nelson Chow

www.ncda.biz

P. 224

NICOLE BLAIR
Nicole Blair

www.nicoleblair.com

P. 236

ODELIA BARZILAY INTERIOR DESIGN
Odelia Barzilay

www.odelia-barzilay.com

P. 246

OSLOTRE
Oslotre Team

www.oslotre.no

P. 256

PETER BRAITHWAITE STUDIO
Peter Braithwaite

www.peterbraithwaitestudio.com

P. 264

STANAĆEV GRANADOS
Nataša Stanaćev, Manu Granados

www.stanacev-granados.com

P. 276

STUDIO HEYA
Nathalie Franquebalme

www.studioheya.com

P. P. 286

STUDIO ONU
Kuba Tomaszczyk

www.onustudio.com

P. 296

STUDIO RAZAVI ARCHITECTURE
Alireza Razavi

www.studiorazavi.com

P. 310

STUDIO STOOKS
Ash Stucken
Collaborator: Miranda Geiger

www.studiostooks.com.au

P. 320

ZOZAYA ARQUITECTOS
Daniel Zozaya, Enrique Zozaya

www.zozayaarquitectos.com

PROPORTIO·
INTUITION·
Van Gogh